Nurse Assistant Test Preparation

by

Wanda Smith, RN, BSN

Brady/Prentice Hall
Upper Saddle River, New Jersey 07458

Library of Congress Cataloging-in-Publication Data

Smith, Wanda, RN
    Nurse assistant test preparation / by Wanda Smith
        p.   cm. -- (Brady/Prentice Hall test prep series)
    ISBN 0-8359-4925-7
    1. Nurses' aides--Examinations, questions, etc. 2. Nurses' aides--
Outlines, syllabi, etc. 3. Care of the sick--Examinations.
questions, etc. 4. Care of the sick--Outlines, syllabi, etc.
I. Series.
    [DNLM: 1. Nurses' Aides--examination questions.   WY 18 S663n
1995]
    RT84.S64 1995
610.73'06'98--dc20
DNLM/DLC
for Library of Congress   94-35572
                                      CIP

With great appreciation the author would like to extend a special thanks to Prentice Hall for the golden opportunity to be part of the enhancement of the quality of health care providers. To the authors at Prentice Hall, Rose B. Schniedman, Susan S. Lambert, Barbara R. Wander, Connie Wills, and Judith B. Eighmy, thanks for the use of the illustrations necessary to complete this book. A special thanks to my husband Denny Smith for the love, emotional support, and encouragement provided throughout this endeavor; to my mother Mercedes Freeny for love and emotional support; and to my sister Cavon Brown for her advice and guidance. Recognition is also given to White's Computerized Secretarial Service for word processing service.

Dedicated: In loving memory of George Elbert Freeny, my dad.

An American BookWorks Corporation Project
Contributing Editor: *Trudy Gensheimer, R.N.*
Acquisitions Editor: *Barbara Krawiec*
Director of Manufacturing & Production: *Bruce Johnson*
Manufacturing Buyer: *Ilene Sanford*
Editorial Assistant: *Louise Fullam*
Formatting/Page Make-up: *American BookWorks Corp./Eureka! Design*
Printer/Binder: *Banta Company (Harrisonburg)*

© 1995 by Prentice-Hall, Inc.
Upper Saddle River, New Jersey 07458

Printed in the United States of America
10 9 8 7 6 5

ISBN 0-8359-4925-7

Prentice-Hall International (UK) Limited, *London*
Prentice-Hall of Australia Pty. Limited, *Sidney*
Prentice-Hall Canada, Inc., *Toronto*
Prentice-Hall Hispanoamericana, S.A., *Mexico*
Prentice-Hall of India Private Limited, *New Delhi*
Prentice-Hall of Japan, Inc., *Tokyo*
Pearson Education Asia Pte. Ltd., *Singapore*
Editora Prentice-Hall do Brasil, Ltda., *Rio de Janeiro*

Contents

Preface

This first edition of Nurse Assistant Test Preparation has been specially designed to aid you, the nurse assistant, in the successful completion of the Competency Evaluation Program mandated by the Omnibus Budget Reconciliation Act (OBRA). As of April 1, 1992, each nurse assistant must be certified for practice.

The author's objective is to enhance the competency level of the practicing nurse assistant. To achieve this goal, a detailed, easy-to-read, and easy-to-understand study text has been developed to guide the candidate through the testing process with as little anxiety as possible. The content has been simplified and divided into 27 chapters (with hundreds of questions) to include the following:

- Introduction to the Competency Evaluation Program with answers to commonly asked questions.
- Helpful hints to reduce pretesting anxiety.
- Health care institution policies.
- Basic nursing care concepts
- Basic resident care skills.
- Residents rights with emphasis on privacy.
- Communication skills.
- Safety and infection control.
- Physical needs.
- Psychosocial needs.
- Nutritional needs.
- Human body and conditions
- Medical and legal terminology.
- Vital signs.
- Admission, discharge, and rehabilitation.
- Death and dying.
- Home health care.
- Observation, reporting, and documentation.
- Positioning and transferring techniques.

Nurse Assistant Test Preparation has an outline preceding each chapter, with questions formulated to clarify the topic outline. Answers at the end of each chapter enhance the candidate's understanding of the nursing concepts.

Discussion of commonly performed procedures with illustrations and questions and answers, will validate the candidate's comprehension of the step-by-step performance skills. Individual sections present separate procedures to allow complete understanding of each skill.

The author recommends that each nurse assistant candidate thoroughly study and complete this text. Completion of this text will increase your level of nursing awareness and ensure successful results in future testing. The author of this text is a registered nurse and has been a nursing educator for the past 16 years. Her expertise has assisted hundreds of nursing candidates receive their certifications and licenses in the field of nursing. Her experience as a nursing educator, a former state health facilities evaluator of long-term care facilities, and as a member of committees formulating test preparation, has formed the background for the wide variety of vital information in this test preparation text.

Introduction

The Competency Evaluation Program requirements enhances the quality of care provided by the certified nurse assistant. The certification as a nurse assistant is a very important document that can make the difference in your ability to retain your present employment or obtain future employment. Certification as a nurse assistant is also a requirement for entry into higher-level nursing programs. Taking advantage of this preparation text can increase your chances of success in your present employment and in your future nursing endeavors.

Preparation for the Competency Evaluation Program should be a goal of each candidate, and this text will assist you to accomplish this goal. It will allow mental entry into the actual testing process. Each chapter has been carefully outlined with the questions, and answers, commonly used by testing organizations. Procedures most frequently performed in your role as a nurse assistant with relevant questions and answers are also included. Review each chapter thoroughly and read the questions carefully. The candidate should be careful to read the questions and not read any additional information into the questions. Each question should be handled on an individual basis. The key focus areas, such as infection control, safety, communications, independence, dignity, privacy, and observations should be incorporated throughout the testing process.

The author would also like to welcome all beginning nurse assistant candidates to the field of nursing and to wish you luck and success on the successful completion of the Competency Evaluation Program.

COMPETENCY EVALUATION PROGRAM

As of April 1, 1992, Omnibus Budget Reconciliation Act (OBRA) required all nurse assistants to successfully complete a state-approved training program. They must also successfully complete a state-approved Competency Evaluation Program (CEP). The Competency Evaluation Program must include both skills performance or demonstrations and an oral or written examination.

A nurse assistant's ability to perform tasks can be evaluated by a demonstration of skills he or she has learned. A nurse assistant's knowledge of certain concepts relating to the care of the resident can be tested by a written or oral exam. Candidates are given three opportunities to successfully complete the examination. After three unsuccessful attempts, candidates are required to repeat the nurse assistant's training program.

The purpose of these requirements is to ensure that the nurse assistant has the education, practical knowledge, and skills required to provide care to the resident.

TEST APPLICATION AND FEE

Application forms must be obtained from your institution of instruction. The approved schools or facilities have been issued an approval number which must be obtained from your instructor.

The application must be completed and signatures of the candidate and instructor must be included. No application will be accepted at the time of testing if the application is not completed. Two forms of identification, one with a photograph must be brought to the testing site on the day of the examination.

The examination fee is approximately $85.00, which should be paid at least three weeks in advance. These fees may vary from state to state.

Be sure to verify the pre-examination process and fee requirements with your local state testing organization.

TESTING ORGANIZATIONS

In California the designated state testing organizations are the Chancellor's Office of California Community Colleges and the American Red Cross. Other states utilizing the American Red Cross are Hawaii, Montana, Pennsylvania, New Jersey and Massachusetts. Contact your State Board of Nursing for your local state testing organizations.

RECIPROCITY

Certified nurse assistants from other states may apply with the local State Board of Nursing for reciprocity. Reciprocity is not automatic and is dependant on each state's guidelines.

CHALLENGE

You may qualify to challenge the Competency Evaluation Program if you meet the following requirements:

- You are registered in an approved licensed nurse program and have completed the credit-hour requirements of your state's nurse assistant program.
- You are a graduate nurse from another country with transcripts to verify completed course work.
- You are a medically trained veteran with verification of training and work experience.

These requirements may vary from state to state. Contact your local State Board of Nursing for requirements in your state.

PRIOR CONVICTIONS

If you have any prior convictions, you must notify the State Board of Nursing in writing of the circumstances. Notifications should include copies of the disposition of your case and be filed at least six weeks in advance of the projected enrollment date.

The board must have sufficient time to evaluate circumstances and give approval in writing. An approval will be sent to you and must be attached to your examination application at the time of testing.

No candidate will be allowed to participate in the examination process without the State Board of Nursing official approval form.

Examination Preparation

HELPFUL HINTS

1. Review all information pertaining to nurse assistant training. Complete the questions in this book and review the questions you were unable to answer correctly.

2. Dress appropriately. Uniforms aren't mandatory; however, a clean, white, comfortable uniform will help you to look professional.

3. Get a good night's rest to ensure a comfortable day of testing.

4. Consume a well-balanced diet so hunger won't cause you to become fatigued and unable to perform at your best.

5. Bring the completed application and two forms of identification, one with a photograph.

6. Leave home early enough to allow arrival 30 minutes prior to the examination.

7. Wear a watch with a second hand.

8. If English is a problem, remember to bring an English interpreted dictionary.

9. Be calm and try to relax.

10. Remember that the examination is on information you were taught in your nurse assistant's training program.

Examination Process

PERFORMANCE SKILLS

Each candidate will be required to perform at least five nursing tasks. These tasks will include routine procedures taught to you during your nurse assistant's training program. During the performance of your skills you are required to include the following principles:

Safety

Infection control

Independence

Dignity

Communications

Privacy

Observations

Examples of tasks you may be required to perform:
    Vital signs
    Handwashing
    Personal care
    Grooming
    Bedmaking
    Positioning
    Gait belt transfers
    Heimlich maneuver
    Measuring height in bed
    Height and weight/upright scale
    Applying elastic stocking
    Applying gloves, mask and gown
    Range of motion
    Assisting with elimination
    Intake and output
    Assisting with nutrition
    Observation skills
    Reporting and recording

The above skills will be evaluated by registered nurses. Skills selections may vary from state to state.

WRITTEN EXAMINATION

A written multiple-choice examination is standard. An alternate method of testing may be available upon request. Examination key focus areas include:
    Observation and reporting
    Vital signs
    Personal care
    Safety measures
    Infection control
    Communications
    Nutrition and diets
    Abbreviations
    Skin care
    Positioning
    Transfer skills
    Restorative care
    Signs and symptoms
    Resident's rights
    Death and dying
The examination will consist of approximately 60 questions, and a score of 70 is mandatory to achieve a passing score. The number of questions and scoring may vary from state to state.

Same-day results may be available through some testing organizations. Contact your local state testing organization for the time frame of examination results.

CERTIFICATION

Upon successful completion of the Competency Evaluation Program, allow four to ten weeks to receive state certification. Renewal of certification is required every two years. Completion of continuing education classes (CEUs) is mandatory. Each renewal applicant must complete 48 hours of CEUs to receive certification.

Contact your local State Board of Nursing for renewal requirements.

Preparing for a Standardized Test

Welcome to the world of standardized test taking, which can often be a very anxiety-producing event. It is likely that you've taken a standardized test before in earlier stages of your schooling. It should not be difficult for you to do well on this kind of test if you know the material. It is because of what this kind of test often represents - getting promoted, going to college, receiving a license- that you feel so much pressure.

This book is designed to help reduce some of that stress. It guides you, chapter by chapter, through the various sections of the actual examination, and provides you with a simple and easy way to study for the exam.

First, the questions in this book have been written to approximate the types of questions you will find on the actual examination, and to present the same level of difficulty that you would find in the questions. In this way you will have a strong sense of what types of questions will appear on the actual examination, and therefore you will be less intimidated when you open your test booklet.

Second, there is no attempt here to try to trick you in any way. The chapters are broken down according to the specific test requirements. In this way, you will not only practice answering questions in each subject area, but you will be able to evaluate your strengths and weaknesses. When you have answered the questions in a specific chapter, you can then grade yourself. By breaking down your score into a percentage, you can then determine if you need to spend more time studying that chapter. In case you've forgotten how to calculate a percentage, use the following formula:

Number of questions correct/Total number of questions = Percentage correct

If you received a score below 85 percent in any one section, it would be helpful to go back and review that chapter. You can either review those questions that you answered incorrectly, or go back to your textbook or review book for additional study. Don't forget, you can always ask your instructor for help, too.

Third, the questions that were selected for inclusion in this book have been designed to help you actually learn the material that you might not already know and to reinforce your previous knowledge. By answering the questions sequentially and then checking the answers, you will be able to determine what you already know and what areas require additional study. Read the answers carefully, since they have been written to help you learn, not just to provide you with the correct answer.

This book is not designed just to help you score high on an exam. Although there are some people who can score well on any type of standardized examination, without the basic knowledge of the material it would be very difficult for most people to do well.

HOW TO ANSWER MULTIPLE-CHOICE QUESTIONS

Most multiple-choice questions follow a pattern, and you will be able to determine what that is after answering enough questions in this book. Normally there is only one correct answer. The other choices are wrong.

However, included among those incorrect answers are choices that are designed to distract you. They are wrong—even though they are close to the correct choice. They may be partially correct. But do not be misled!

The best way to answer a question is to read it carefully and try to answer it before actually looking at the choices. If you've paid attention throughout your schooling, you may well know the answer immediately. Then look at the choices. If the answer you thought of is one of the choices, accept it, and fill in the appropriate blank on your answer key.

If you do not know the answer immediately, it is possible that when you read the answer choices one will jump out at you. Again, that is probably the correct answer.

When your mind draws a blank, your only choice is to work backward and try to find the answer by the process of elimination. Cross off those that you know are incorrect. If you are lucky, you may narrow down the choices to three, or even two. Then reread the question. Look for key words or phrases that may be included in the question and worded differently in the answers.

Be careful of words like Never, Except, and Always. They are trick questions and may force you into making incorrect choices.

Finally, don't second-guess yourself. Questions are normally specific and direct. They don't say one thing while meaning another. The typical "second-guesser" reads too much into the question. For example, look at the following multiple-choice question:

1. The name of the president's wife is
   A. Barbara
   B. Betty
   C. Nancy
   D. Hillary
   E. Ruth

As this book goes to press, the president of the United States is Bill Clinton. His wife's name is Hillary. The correct answer is D. You knew that, didn't you?

However, the second-guesser immediately tries to look at the copyright date of the exam and thinks "Was George Bush president when this exam was written? The test preparers really must mean that Barbara is the correct answer. Or perhaps Ruth is the name of the president of the school that I'm attending. What should I do?"

Don't read into the question. Just read the question for its "face value."

There are several forms of multiple-choice questions that you might encounter, and although their technical names are unimportant to you, it is important for you to understand their forms.

Type 1. This is the traditional type of question that is most often employed on multiple-choice examinations. It consists of a question and four or five choices.

1. United States Supreme Court justices are appointed for life primarily because such long terms of office:
   A. Lessen political interference in judicial decisions.
   B. Allow the justices time to gain experience in their jobs.
   C. Reward political supporters with secure jobs.
   D. Save expenses caused by frequent changes in office.
   E. Develop skills.

The correct answer is A. Answers B and E are similar, and it is obvious that if a justice doesn't have the necessary skills to begin with, he or she shouldn't be appointed to such an important position. Answer D is also far-fetched, since justices are appointed and there are no large election expenses spent by a justice to gain that appointment. Answer C might almost seem correct, given the nature of congressional hearings that have taken place in the last several years to appoint new justices, which surely take on political overtones. But answer C is the opposite of answer A, and one need only pick up a newspaper during a congressional hearing for a new justice to understand the apolitical nature of a Supreme Court justice.

Type 2. This is a type of question that requires you to read the choices closely. It is the "Except" question.

2. Each of the following women were presidential first ladies, EXCEPT:
   A. Barbara Bush
   B. Betty Ford
   C. Nancy Reagan
   D. Hillary Clinton
   E. Amy Carter

The correct answer is E. I hope you recognized that Amy Carter is former President Jimmy Carter's daughter. His wife's name is Rosalind.

Type 3. The combination question is a little more difficult. In this type of question, you have to select combinations of choices.

3. Of the following, which first ladies were married to Republican presidents?
   A. Barbara Bush and Hillary Clinton
   B. Barbara Bush and Nancy Reagan
   C. Betty Ford and Rosalind Carter
   D. Hillary Clinton and Tipper Gore
   E. Nancy Reagan and Rosalind Carter

The correct answer is B. Hillary Clinton and Rosalind Carter were first ladies in Democratic administrations, and Tipper Gore is the wife of a vice president.

Type 4. Another type of combination question is similar to the above question, but has multiple parts.

4. Presidents of Democratic administrations include:
    1. Ronald Reagan
    2. Harry S Truman
    3. Jimmy Carter
    4. Bill Clinton
    5. George Bush
        A. 1, 5
        B. 2, 3, 4
        C. 2, 4
        D. 3
        E. 4, 5

The correct answer is B. Truman, Carter, and Clinton are all Democrats. Any choice with Reagan or Bush must be incorrect because they are Republicans. Choices C and D are not wrong, but they are incomplete. Only answer B is complete.

Type 5. The familiar matching items questions are often easy. They may consist of multiple columns or a heading, a diagram, sets of items, and so on, to be matched with a list of choices.

5. Match the president with the appropriate first lady.
    A. George Bush   1. Nancy
    B. Bill Clinton   2. Bess
    C. Ronald Reagan   3. Pat
    D. Harry S Truman   4. Hillary
    E. Richard Nixon   5. Barbara

The correct answers are: A-5, B-4, C-1, D-2, E-5. If you didn't remember Harry Truman's wife Bess, you should have figured it out by the process of elimination.

Remember to take your time when answering a question. If you don't understand the question the first time you read it, read it again. If the correct answer doesn't pop into your head once you've read the question and before you've read the choices, start eliminating those choices that you feel are absolutely incorrect. In the end, you may have to guess. But if you've been studying for the exam, if you've paid attention in class, and if you've read your textbook, even your guess will be an educated guess.

Good luck!

Part One:

Written Examination

with

Questions and Answers

1

Various Health Environments

I. Health care providers
   A. Purpose
   B. Types
   C. Functions

II. Method of payment
   A. Medicare
   B. Medicaid
   C. DRGs

III. Health care receivers
   A. Variations

IV. Health care team members
   A. Purpose
   B. Types
   C. Functions

V. Health care environments
   A. Departments
      1. Types
      2. Functions
   B. Specialty areas
      1. Variations
      2. Functions

VI. Health care institution terminology
   A. Key terms
      1. Admission
      2. Diagnosis
      3. Discharge
      4. Prognosis
      5. Primary nursing
      6. Task oriented
      7. Patient oriented

QUESTIONS

DIRECTIONS: Each question contains four suggested responses. Select the one best response to each question.

ANSWERS: See answers at the end of the questions.

1. The primary purposes of health care institutions are all of the following EXCEPT:
   a. Preventing disease
   b. Promoting individual and community health
   c. Refusing to provide care to the ill or injured
   d. Providing facilities for the education of health workers

2. Which one of the following health care institutions provides emergency room services?
   a. Skilled
   b. Intermediate
   c. Board and care
   d. Hospital

3. The classification of the skilled nursing facility and convalescent hospital is:
   a. Clinic
   b. Hospice care
   c. Long-term care
   d. Home health care

4. A resident must be placed in a facility which provides 24-hour licensed nursing care. Select the appropriate facility.
   a. Skilled
   b. Home health care
   c. Intermediate
   d. Board and care

5. The resident is self-care but requires generalized supervision from a licensed nurse. Select the appropriate facility.
   a. Hospice
   b. Skilled
   c. Intermediate
   d. Board and care

6. The resident is being discharged to his or her environment and requires daily nursing care. Which facility will provide care?
   a. Long-term care
   b. Hospice
   c. Home health care
   d. Board and care

7. Home health nursing care must be ordered by:
   a. Family
   b. Nurse
   c. Physician
   d. Therapist

8. Which health care provider will provide services for a terminally ill resident in the home?
   a. Home health care
   b. Hospice
   c. Long-term care
   d. Hospital

9. The terms in-patient and out-patient refer to:
   a. Clinics
   b. Home health care
   c. Long-term care
   d. Hospital

10. Medicare and Medicaid are health institution payment plans primarily for elderly and:
    a. Rich
    b. Low-income
    c. Veterans
    d. Middle elderly

11. Medicare and Medicaid made health care accessible to the low-income and elderly:
    a. According to diagnostically related groups (DRGs)
    b. According to length of stay
    c. According to family's request
    d. According to resident's request

12. The term "patient" or "resident" refers to:
    a. Workers
    b. Caretakers
    c. Care receivers
    d. Caregivers

13. Which team member is responsible for the smooth operation of the health care institution?
    a. Director of nurses

b. Administrator
c. Supervisor
d. Physician

14. The team member who manages and writes medical orders for the care of each resident is:
    a. Administrator
    b. Director of nurses
    c. Supervisor
    d. Physician

15. The licensed practical nurse (LPN) or licensed vocational nurse (LVN) must work under direct supervision of:
    a. Registered nurse (RN)
    b. Administrator
    c. Physician
    d. Certified nurse assistant

16. The nursing supervisor is responsible for the supervision of all nursing staff **except**:
    a. Director of nurses
    b. Registered nurses
    c. Licensed practical or vocational nurses
    d. Certified nurse assistant

17. Providing inservice and nursing updates to nursing staff is done by:
    a. Director of education
    b. Supervisors
    c. Head nurse
    d. Team leader

18. The term licensed practical or licensed vocational nurse refers to:
    a. Nurse completing one year of nursing training who has passed the state board examination
    b. Nurse completing two years of nursing training who has passed the state board examination
    c. Nurse completing four years of nursing training who has passed state board examination
    d. Nurse completing six months of nursing training

19. The term "orderly" refers to:
    a. RN
    b. LVN

c. LPN
d. NA

20. The nurse assistant reports all resident complaints to the:
    a. Team leader
    b. Head nurse
    c. Physician
    d. Nursing supervisor

21. The nurse assistant's primary function is to:
    a. Administer medications
    b. Provide basic nursing care
    c. Notify physician for orders
    d. Tube feed

22. Select the team member responsible for clerical duties and answering the telephone.
    a. Orderly
    b. Nurse assistant
    c. Supervisor
    d. Ward clerk

23. The health care institution has a variety of departments. Which service issues facility policies and procedures?
    a. Administrative services
    b. Fiscal services
    c. Professional services
    d. General services

24. Physicians are classified as:
    a. Nursing staff
    b. Auxiliary groups
    c. Other professional services
    d. Medical staff

25. Select the specialty area that deals with removal of an organ.
    a. Medicine
    b. Surgery
    c. Neurology
    d. Radiology

26. Which of the following specialty areas would repair a fractured femur?
    a. Obstetrics
    b. Dermatology
    c. Orthopedics
    d. Neurology

27. Which specialty area services a resident complaining of feeling tired (lethargic)?
    a. Gynecology
    b. Internal medicine
    c. Dermatology
    d. Allergy

28. The specialty area dealing with assisting the resident to sleep by administering various forms of gases is which of the following?
    a. Pathology
    b. Cardiology
    c. Anesthesiology
    d. Pediatrics

29. The nurse assistant is providing care to a 10-year-old child. Which service deals with children?
    a. Ophthalmology
    b. Pediatrics
    c. Pathology
    d. Plastic surgery

30. The nurse assistant is providing care to a pregnant resident. The most likely specialty area is:
    a. Orthopedics
    b. Neurology
    c. Obstetrics
    d. Ophthalmology

31. A subspecialty of internal medicine involving the diagnosis and treatment of diseases of the heart and blood vessels is called:
    a. Pathology
    b. Dermatology
    c. Neurology
    d. Cardiology

32. Which service would the nurse assistant have to understand to deal with skin problems?
    a. Dermatology
    b. Pathology
    c. Gastroenterology
    d. Gynecology

33. The nurse assistant is providing care to a resident who has just entered the hospital. This process is called:
    a. Admission
    b. Discharge

    c. Transfer
    d. Coercion

34. During the admission process the nurse assistant will need to obtain the resident's weight. Select the equipment to be used.
    a. Scale
    b. Graduate
    c. Wheelchair
    d. Commode

35. The diagnosis is the reason the resident is in the health care institution. Which team member identifies the diagnosis?
    a. Registered nurse (RN)
    b. Licensed practical nurse (LPN)
    c. Licensed vocational nurse
    d. Physician

36. The process of assisting the resident to leave the health care institution is called:
    a. Transfer
    b. Admission
    c. Discharge
    d. Detention

37. Prognosis is best described as:
    a. Reason resident is hospitalized
    b. Forecast of the outcome of resident's disease
    c. Length of resident's hospital stay
    d. Resident's activity plan

38. Primary nursing care is the responsibility of which team member?
    a. RN
    b. LPN or LVN
    c. Orderly
    d. CNA

39. Select the appropriate term to define nursing care arranged according to what must be done.
    a. Patient-oriented
    b. Primary nursing
    c. Task-oriented
    d. Basic nursing

40. Select the appropriate term to define nursing care arranged according to the total needs of the individual resident.
    a. Functional nursing
    b. Team nursing
    c. Primary nursing
    d. Patient-oriented nursing

Answers

1. c. The five basic functions and purposes of health care institutions are to provide care to the ill and/or injured, to prevent disease, to promote individual and community health, to provide facilities for the education of health workers, and to promote research in the science of medicine.

2. d. One purpose of health care is to provide care for the ill or injured. The hospital is the health care institution providing emergency room services for ill or injured residents.

3. c. Long-term health care is an umbrella that covers many levels of care. Board and care takes in individuals who are usually ambulatory and self-care, but also need supervision with their activities of daily living (ADL). Intermediate care facilities provide unlicensed nursing care with some generalized supervision from a licensed nurse. A skilled nursing facility or convalescent hospital provides care to residents with diagnoses and problems that require the skills of a licensed nurse to regulate their care 24 hours a day.

4. a. Skilled or long-term care facilities provide 24-hour licensed nursing care. The resident generally requires monitoring 24 hours a day. Medication and nutritional needs are important factors. Basic nursing care is provided by the nursing assistant.

5. c. The intermediate care facility provides unlicensed nursing care with some generalized supervision from a licensed nurse.

6. c. The home health agency supervises care in the home until the resident is stable. The resident in the home should receive the same high quality of nursing care given in the health care institution.

7. c. An order is a command, direction or instruction given by a superior requiring obedient execution of a task. In home health care, the physician must order specific nursing care.

8. b. The hospice program allows a dying resident to remain at home and die at home, while receiving professionally supervised care. The home health aide will perform basic nursing care in the home.

9. a. Clinics provide both in-patient and out-patient care.

10. b. Medicare and Medicaid made health care accessible to the elderly, low-income, and disabled. Health insurance made the health care system accessible to workers through job-related benefits.

11. a. The new method of payment to allow elderly, disabled, and low-income people access to medical treatment is by diagnostically related groups (DRGs), not on length of stay. A diagnosis is the physician's determination of what kind of disease or condition a resident or patient has. Diagnoses have been categorized into related groups. Medicare determines the amount it will pay to the health care institution for each group of illnesses or conditions.

12. c. Patient and resident have the same meaning.

13. b. The administrator is totally responsible for the operations of the health care team and all services or departments. The administrator corresponds with department heads to facilitate smooth facility operations.

14. d. The doctor (physician) manages and writes medical orders for the care of each resident and has all medical responsibility.

15. a. In the organization of the health care team, the registered nurse is responsible and must supervise LPNs or LVNs, and the nurse assistant. The registered nurse (RN) is the teacher, adviser and helper to all team members.

16. a. The supervisor is a registered nurse and works under direct supervision of the director of nurses. The director of nurses is responsible for all nursing staff.

17. a. The director of nursing education provides all staff with inservice updates regarding changes in nursing procedures, updates in nursing practice and reinforcement in daily nursing tasks.

18. a. The licensed practical or vocational nurse must complete one year of nursing education and pass the state examination.

19. d. The term "orderly" is another term for nurse assistant, a paraprofessional worker who works under the direction and supervision of the registered nurses and carries out basic bedside nursing functions.

20. a. The nurse assistant reports all resident complaints and other problems to the team leader. The team leader has the knowledge and skills to handle problems in a professional manner.

21. b. The nurse assistant works under direct supervision of the registered nurse and carries out basic bedside nursing functions.

22. d. The ward clerk works at the desk of the nurse's station and does clerical work, answers the telephone, helps to direct traffic on the floor, and fills out requisition slips.

23. a. The personnel department falls under administrative services. Personnel will provide you with the facilities' policies and procedures along with your job specifications.

24. d. The physicians are a part of the medical staff.

25. b. The diagnosis and treatment of disease by surgical means, without limitations to special organs.

26. c. Orthopedics deals with diagnosis and treatment of disorders and diseases of muscular and skeletal systems.

27. b. Internal medicine deals with the diagnosis and nonsurgical treatment of illnesses of adults. The physician in this specialty is called an internist.

28. c. Anesthesiology is concerned with administering various forms of anesthesia in operations or diagnostic procedures to cause loss of feeling or sensation. The physician is called an anesthesiologist.

29. b. Pediatrics deals with prevention, diagnosis and treatment of children's diseases. The physician is called a pediatrician.

30. c. Obstetrics deals with the care of a woman during pregnancy, childbirth, and the period immediately following. The doctor is called an obstetrician.

31. d. Cardiology deals with internal medicine involving the diagnosis and treatment of diseases of the heart and blood vessels. The physician is called a cardiologist.

32. a. Dermatology deals with the diagnosis and treatment of disorders of the skin. The physician is called a dermatologist.

33. a. Admission covers the administrative procedures followed when a person enters the health care institution and becomes an in-patient. The covered period is from the time the patient enters the door of the hospital until the patient is settled in his or her room.

34. a. A portable balance scale is used to weigh ambulatory residents. There are several types of scales. For example, residents who are unable to stand can use the chair scale, bed scale, or wheelchair scale. Some institutions have scales with bars to assist residents in standing straight and to keep them from falling.

35. d. The physician determines the disease or condition of the resident. The physician also writes the treatment plan during the hospital stay and is responsible for ordering all nursing care and medication.

36. c. The discharge procedure for helping the residents to leave the health care institution includes teaching them how to care for themselves at home.

37. b. The prognosis is the forecast of the outcome of the resident's disease or condition. Various examples are good, fair, or poor.

38. a. The registered Nurse (RN) is the caregiver in primary nursing care. This is a resident-oriented method of organizing the health care team. The registered nurses are responsible for the total nursing care of the resident.

39. c. Task-oriented nursing care is arranged according to what must be done. The team leader assigns the patient care to the team members.

40. d. Patient-oriented nursing care is arranged according to the total needs of the individual patient or resident.

2

Nurse Assistant's Role and Responsibility

DIRECTIONS: Each question contains four suggested responses. Select the one best response to each question.

ANSWERS: See answers at the end of the questions.

1. The primary function of the nurse assistant is:
   a. Basic nursing care
   b. Daily record of medication
   c. Reporting to physician
   d. Supervising staff

2. All are functions of the nurse assistant EXCEPT:
   a. Bathing the resident
   b. Reporting problems
   c. Documenting
   d. Diagnosis interpretation with family

3. All of the following are examples of personal care EXCEPT:
   a. Oral hygiene
   b. Shaving
   c. Nail care
   d. Vital signs

4. Nail care, hair care, bathing, and shaving are examples of:
   a. Personal care
   b. Early morning care
   c. Afternoon care
   d. Hour of sleep care

5. How often does the unconscious resident receive mouth care?
   a. Twice each shift
   b. Every three hours
   c. Every two hours
   d. Once each shift

6. How should the resident's dentures be stored?
   a. No water
   b. Cold water
   c. Warm water
   d. Hot water

7. How often should the nurse assistant bathe the older resident?
   a. Once a week
   b. Twice a week
   c. Three times a week
   d. Four times a week

8. The accurate water temperature for a tub bath is:
   a. 105° F
   b. 110° F
   c. 120° F
   d. 130° F

9. Which procedure requires a doctor's order?
   a. Restraints
   b. Vital signs
   c. Range of motion
   d. Linen change

10. The nurse assistant can use all of the following shaving equipment EXCEPT:
    a. Straight razor
    b. Shaving cream
    c. Safety razor
    d. Electric razor

11. In which direction should the nails be trimmed?
    a. Curved
    b. Straight across
    c. V-shaped
    d. One side only

12. Thicker nails are found mainly in which group of residents?
    a. Pediatric
    b. Teenage
    c. Middle-aged
    d. Elderly

13. Which statement is true regarding the autoclave?
    a. Kills all germs on an object
    b. Kills one-fourth of germs on an object
    c. Kills one-half of germs on an object
    d. Kills three-fourths of germs on an object

14. Hand washing is performed how often?
    a. Twice a day
    b. After each resident's care
    c. Six times a day
    d. Before and after each task

15. To increase trust and decrease fear, suspicion, and apprehension on the part of the resident before a procedure, the nurse assistant should:
    a. Wash his or her hands
    b. Pull the curtain
    c. Explain the procedure
    d. Lower the side rail

16. Which condition would the nurse assistant report to the charge nurse?
    a. Wet resident
    b. Normal bowel habits
    c. Cooperative resident
    d. Open redden area

17. Select the appropriate diet for a hypertensive resident.
    a. Regular
    b. Low sodium
    c. No sugar
    d. Bland

18. The following are examples of nutrients EXCEPT:
    a. Carbohydrates
    b. Proteins
    c. Alcohol
    d. Vitamins

19. Which nutritional diet has no dietary restrictions?
    a. Regular
    b. Bland
    c. Diabetic
    d. Soft

20. Sugar *is not* allowed on which diet?
    a. Low residue
    b. Bland
    c. Diabetic
    d. Low sodium

21. The resident *cannot* chew and is at risk of choking. Select appropriate diet.
    a. Regular
    b. Soft
    c. Pureed
    d. High protein

22. An objective observation is all of the following EXCEPT:
    a. What the nurse assistant can see
    b. What the resident states
    c. What the nurse assistant can feel
    d. What the nurse assistant can hear

23. An example of an subjective observation is:
    a. Edema
    b. Red eyes
    c. Rash
    d. Headache

24. Select the appropriate term for swelling
    a. Enema
    b. Cyanosis
    c. Edema
    d. Jaundice

25. Which statement should the nurse assistant understand regarding observation of residents?
    a. Observation is only done by licensed nurses.
    b. Observation begins at the first sight of the resident and ends at discharge.
    c. Abnormal observations are not reported.
    d. Observation is not a continuous process.

26. The nurse assistant must report abnormal observations to which team member?
    a. Charge nurse
    b. Administrator
    c. Physician
    d. Supervisor

27. Select appropriate information regarding reporting observations.
    a. First name and room number
    b. Room number and bed number
    c. Resident's full name only
    d. Resident's name, room number, and bed number

28. Select the appropriate term for the measuring of body heat.
    a. Respiration
    b. Pulse
    c. Temperature
    d. Blood pressure

29. Which instrument measures body heat?
    a. Watch
    b. Thermometer
    c. Stethoscope
    d. Sphygmomanometer

30. Select the term which best describes how fast the heart is beating.
    a. Temperature
    b. Respiration
    c. Pulse
    d. Blood pressure

31. The process of inhaling and exhaling is called:
    a. Respiration
    b. Aspiration
    c. Expiration
    d. Defecation

32. Which instrument measures the force of the blood flowing through the arteries?
    a. Thermometer
    b. Watch
    c. Stethoscope
    d. Sphygmomanometer

33. Select the best description of a stethoscope.
    a. Collecting device
    b. Listening device
    c. Eating device
    d. Speaking device

34. All of the following are used in elimination EXCEPT:
    a. Bedpan
    b. Urinal
    c. Emesis basin
    d. Portable commode

35. All of the following are observations of the incontinent resident EXCEPT:
    a. Wet bed
    b. Soiled clothing
    c. Dry bed
    d. Irritated skin

36. The primary function of the indwelling catheter is:
    a. Drainage of the bladder
    b. Drainage of the stomach
    c. Drainage of the colon
    d. Relief of flatus

37. Encouraging the elderly resident to assist in activities of daily living promotes:
    a. Dependence
    b. Independence
    c. Deterioration
    d. Depression

38. The following are part of the nurse assistant dress code EXCEPT:
    a. Uniform according to facility policy
    b. Polished nonskid-soled shoes
    c. Large dangling earrings
    d. Identification badge

39. All of the following are qualities of the nurse assistant EXCEPT:
    a. Considerate
    b. Trustworthy
    c. Honest
    d. Uncontrolled temper

40. All of the following qualify the nurse assistant to take the Competency Evaluation Program (state examination) EXCEPT:
    a. Completion of a state-approved nurse assistant training program
    b. Expired certification—no employment in the last 24 months
    c. Graduate training
    d. Non-nursing training

41. The nurse assistant receives certification from which agency?
    a. Training school
    b. Red Cross
    c. Chancellor of colleges
    d. State Board of Nursing

42. Select the correct renewal requirements for the certified nurse assistant (CNA).
    a. Every year
    b. Every two years
    c. Every three years
    d. Every five years

43. The following are examples of ethical behavior EXCEPT:
    a. Uncooperativeness
    b. Confidentiality
    c. Accuracy
    d. Dependability

Answers

1. a. The nurse assistant assists the nurse in supplying nursing care and services to the resident.

2. d. Resident information is confidential. Do not discuss resident information with another resident about another, relatives and friends of the resident, visitors to the hospital, the news media, fellow workers (except when in a conference), or your own relatives and friends.

3. d. Personal care is bathing the body, cleaning the mouth, shaving the face, trimming and cleaning the nails, makeup, and dressing. Vitals signs are not part of personal care.

4. a. Personal care is grooming which includes oral hygiene, nail care, hair care, shaving, makeup, and dressing.

5. c. The unconscious resident should receive oral hygiene every two hours in order to maintain moisture in the mouth. Unconscious residents are generally mouth breathers, causing oral membranes to become extremely dry.

6. b. The dentures are to be placed in the resident's mouth or they can be stored overnight in cold water in a denture cup.

7. b. The older resident should be bathed twice a week. More frequent bathing may further dry the skin.

8. a. Tub bath water temperature is 105° F and should be tested with a bath thermometer.

9. a. The doctor must write an order for the application of restraints. Vital signs, linen change, and range of motion are nursing measures. These are procedures done routinely and when the nurse thinks it necessary.

10. a. The nurse assistant should not use a straight razor. This type of razor is unsafe for the resident. An electrical razor can be used if the resident *is not* receiving oxygen, but a safety razor is generally used.

11. b. The nails should be trimmed straight across and jagged or sharp edges should be smoothed with an emery board to prevent cutting the skin surrounding the nail.

12. d. Elderly residents have thicker nails that are trimmed more easily after soaking.

13. a. When an object is free of all germs or microorganisms, it is sterile. The autoclave sterilizes objects.

14. d. Hand washing must be done before and after each nursing task.

15. c. Good communications practice includes a simple explanation of any procedure. This can decrease fear and suspicion in a resident and can increase trust and cooperation.

16. d. An open redden area is a stage 2 decubitus and requires medical attention. All changes in a resident's condition, appearance, and behavior are to be reported promptly and recorded.

17. b. Certain diagnoses, such as hypertension, have various diet restrictions. The salt increases blood pressure. No salt is allowed in the diet.

18. c. Nutrients are divided into specific classes: carbohydrates, proteins, fats, vitamins, minerals, and water.

19. a. The regular diet has no dietary restrictions. This diet is for residents who do not need special diets.

20. c. Residents with diabetes are on a special diet. Sugar will be eliminated and artificial sweeteners or fruit juices will be substituted.

21. c. The resident who cannot chew and who is at high risk for choking may be placed on a pureed diet. Most food is placed in a blender and reduced to almost a liquid state so that it requires no chewing.

22. b. An objective observation is looking, listening to sounds (such as wheezing, coughing and choking), touching, and

smelling; in other words, what the nurse assistant can see.

23. d. Subjective observations are signs and symptoms that can be felt and described only by the resident. Examples are pain, nausea, dizziness, ringing in the ears, or a headache.

24. c. Fluid can be held in body tissue, causing the tissue to swell. Abnormal swelling of a part of the body by fluid is called edema. Usually the swelling is in the ankles, legs, hands, or abdomen.

25. b. Observation of the resident is a continuous process. Observing begins the first time you meet a resident and ends when the resident is discharged from the health care institution.

26. a. All changes in a resident's condition, appearance, and behavior are to be reported promptly to the charge nurse.

27. d. Write down the resident's name, room number, and bed number. This is done to ensure the charge nurse has the right resident.

28. c. Body temperature is a measurement of the amount of heat in the body. The balance between the heat produced and the heat lost is the body temperature. The normal body temperature is 98° F or 37° C.

29. b. A thermometer is used to measure a resident's body heat.

30. c. The pulse is the rhythmic expansion and contraction of the arteries, which can be measured to show how fast the heart is beating.

31. a. Respiration is the process of inhaling (breathing in) and exhaling (breathing out).

32. d. The blood pressure is taken with a sphygmomanometer. This instrument measures the force of the blood flowing through the arteries. This word is a combination of three Greek words: *sphygmo*, meaning pulse; *mano*, meaning pressure; and *meter*, meaning measure.

33. b. The stethoscope is an instrument that allows one to listen to various sounds in the patient's body, such as heartbeat or breathing sounds.

34. c. The bed pan, urinal, and bedside commode are used for collection of stool and urine. The emesis basin is used to catch materials the resident spits out, vomits, or expectorates.

35. c. The incontinent resident has no control of bowel or bladder. The bed of an incontinent resident gets soiled quite frequently and must be changed. A wet bed, soiled clothing, and irritated skin are seen quite frequently in the incontinent resident.

36. a. The indwelling catheter is a thin sterile tube inserted through the resident's urethra into the bladder. The purpose is to drain the urine from the bladder. The catheter is connected to a closed urinary draining system.

37. b. Promoting independence is encouraging the resident to assist in activities of daily living (ADL), such as dressing, combing the hair, feeding, and toileting, if able. This decreases dependency on the nurse assistant.

38. c. Never wear jewelry, such as large, dangling earrings, bracelets or pendants; small stud earrings, wedding bands and a watch with a second hand can be worn.

39. d. The temper should be controlled at all times. The nurse assistant should be honest, trustworthy, gracious, polite, considerate, tactful, sensitive, sympathetic, and patient.

40. d. To obtain certification as a nurse assistant, you must successfully complete an approved nurse assistant training program and pass the federal competency evaluation exam.

41. d. The state certification card will be issued upon receipt of the examination results.

42. b. The CNA must renew certification every two years on the date of birth.

43. a. Ethical behavior is being cooperative, accurate, and dependable and keeping resident information confidential.

3

Resident's Rights and Communication

DIRECTIONS: Each question contains four suggested responses. Select the one best response to each question.

ANSWERS: See answers at the end of the questions.

1. The Resident's Bill of Rights is best described as:
   a. A list of resident's rules and services regulated by the local police department
   b. Specific guidelines for the resident's treatment, services and expectations regulated by federal and state government
   c. A list of resident's rules decided by the health care providers
   d. Rules and regulations decided by the family members

2. Select the appropriate actions of the nursing assistant to promote the resident's privacy rights.
   a. Explanation of the bath procedure
   b. Reporting the bath to the charge nurse
   c. Closing the curtain before the bath
   d. Allowing the resident to assist with the bath

3. Which of the following actions by the nurse assistant would demonstrate confidentiality?
   a. Allowing family and friends to review the resident's health record
   b. Allowing roommate to review the resident's health record
   c. Allowing the media to review the resident's health record
   d. Allowing nurses, physicians, and therapists to review the resident's health record

4. The nurse assistant should understand which of the following statements regarding Notice of Rights and Services?
   a. The facility has the right to refuse treatment to the in-house residents.
   b. The resident has the right to refuse treatment and to participate in experimental research.
   c. The nurse assistant has the right to refuse services to the resident.
   d. The facility decides the rights of the resident.

5. The resident refuses personal care. Which one of the following should the nurse assistant do?
   a. Ignore the resident
   b. Force the resident physically
   c. Report the problem to the charge nurse
   d. Verbally threaten the resident

6. Referring to the resident as "pops" or "grandma" is a violation of which of the resident's rights?
   a. Dignity
   b. Independence
   c. Privacy
   d. Free choice

7. Which statement is true regarding the resident's funds?
   a. The resident's personal funds must be managed by the health care institution.
   b. The physician controls the resident's funds.
   c. The nurse assistant can manage the resident's personal funds.
   d. The resident's personal funds are not to be deposited in the health care institution's account.

8. All of the following are true regarding the resident's freedom of choice EXCEPT:
   a. The resident has the right to select appropriate clothing to wear.
   b. The resident has the right to be informed in advance about care and treatment.
   c. The resident has the right to be involved in the planning of care.
   d. The resident must be assigned a personal physician by the health care institution.

9. The resident complains to the charge nurse of dissatisfaction with the nursing care. Select the appropriate term.
   a. Incident
   b. Accident
   c. Grievance
   d. Summary

10. Which statement is true regarding telephone rights of the resident?
    a. Telephone conversations are monitored.

b. Telephones are available for the resident's use after 6:00 p.m.

c. Telephones are available.

d. Telephones with privacy and regular access are available.

11. All of the following statements are true about a resident's mail EXCEPT:

a. The resident has the right to send mail.

b. The resident has the right to receive mail.

c. The resident has the right to unopened mail.

d. The resident has the right to stationery and postage at the expense of the facility.

12. Food, shelter, clothing, love, and security are best described as:

a. Basic needs

b. Spiritual needs

c. Cultural needs

d. Psychosocial needs

13. Activity of daily living (ADL) skills are best described as:

a. Physical needs

b. Cultural needs

c. Psychosocial needs

d. Spiritual needs

14. resident's preferences in food, clothing, and lifestyles are described best as:

a. Cultural needs

b. Physical needs

c. Psychosocial needs

d. Basic needs

15. Which statement is true regarding religious beliefs?

a. The nurse assistant can impose his or her religious beliefs on the residents.

b. Each resident has a right to his or her own religious beliefs.

c. Religious beliefs are not recognized in the health care setting.

d. Residents cannot discuss religious beliefs with the nurse assistant.

16. An example of effective communication with the resident is best described as:

a. Listening to and understanding the resident's total complaint

b. Assuming the understanding of the resident's complaint

c. Partially understanding the resident's complaint

d. Rejection of the resident's complaint

17. Effective skills for verbal communication with the resident are all of the following EXCEPT:

a. Clear speech

b. Moderate voice tone

c. Simple questions and answers

d. Using medical terminology

18. All of the following are forms of body language communication EXCEPT:

a. Expressions

b. Gestures

c. Touch

d. Speech

19. An example of a sensory impaired resident is one who is:

a. Blind

b. Obese

c. Hypertensive

d. Nonambulatory

20. Which type of resident should be evacuated first during a facility fire?

a. Ambulatory

b. Blind

c. Wheelchair bound

d. Diabetic

21. The clock method is used to describe food position for which types of residents?

a. Blind residents

b. Paralyzed residents

c. Nonspeaking residents

d. Deaf residents

22. A family member is upset and states, "I am concerned about my mother's care." Select the appropriate response by the nurse assistant.

a. "Would you like to discuss the concerns?"

b. "You would need to speak to the resident's physician."

c. "All of the residents receive the same nursing care."

d. "Would you like to speak to the nurse in charge?"

23. Regarding the team concept, how should the nurse assistant respond to the resident's call signal of a coworker?
   a. Answer the call signal, perform the task and tell the coworker what was done.
   b. Answer the call signal and tell the coworker the resident would like the bedpan.
   c. Don't answer the call signal and allow the coworker to answer.
   d. Each nurse assistant is responsible for answering his or her own call signals.

24. A coworker requests your assistance in performing a task. Select the appropriate response.
   a. "No, I'm too busy."
   b. "Each nurse assistant is responsible for his or her own residents."
   c. "Allow me a moment to secure the resident I am caring for."
   d. "I'll assist you when I have completed my assignment."

25. The charge nurse assigns the nurse assistant responsibility for an additional resident. Select the appropriate action of the nurse assistant.
   a. Accept the resident and provide care.
   b. Accept the resident and verbalize frustration to the resident.
   c. Threaten to go home ill.
   d. Secretly add the resident to a coworker's assignment.

26. All of the following statements are true regarding the nurse assistant's breaks and lunch period EXCEPT:
   a. Nurse assistants relieve each other during breaks.
   b. The charge nurse should be notified before leaving for a break.
   c. Breaks and lunch are not required.
   d. Breaks and lunch are mandatory.

27. Mistakenly, the nurse assistant is assigned four additional residents. Select the appropriate action by the nurse assistant.
   a. Discuss the mistake with the four residents.
   b. Discuss the mistake with the other nurse assistants.

   c. Discuss the mistake with the charge nurse.
   d. Discuss the mistake with the supervisor.

28. All of the following are rights of the resident EXCEPT:
   a. Respect
   b. Self-determination
   c. Undignified existence
   d. Communications

29. Quality of life is best described as:
   a. Promoting the resident's dignity and respect
   b. Making choices for the resident
   c. Not permitting the resident to assist in the plan of care
   d. Discouraging religious beliefs

30. Courtesy is best described as:
   a. Polite
   b. Aggressive
   c. Abusive
   d. Temper

31. Empathy is best described as:
   a. A mental thought of sadness
   b. Exchanging places with the resident
   c. Happiness for the resident
   d. A feeling of separation from the resident

32. All of the following are examples of tact EXCEPT:
   a. Answering the call signal promptly
   b. Encouraging the resident to call for help when needed
   c. Showing frustration each time the resident calls for help
   d. Being considerate at all times

33. Sympathy is best described as:
   a. Happiness
   b. Sorrow
   c. Guilt
   d. Comfort

34. Aggressive behavior is best described as:
   a. Quiet
   b. Demanding
   c. Courteous
   d. Nice

35. Passive behavior is best described as:
   a. Demanding
   b. Rude
   c. Loud
   d. Overly agreeable

36. Assertive behavior is all of the following EXCEPT:
   a. Positive
   b. Firm
   c. Aggressive
   d. Considerate

37. Depression can be described as all of the following EXCEPT:
   a. Disinterest
   b. Low spirits
   c. Sad
   d. Happy

38. All of the following are associated with effective communication EXCEPT:
   a. Nonlistener
   b. Message
   c. Sender
   d. Receiver

39. Explaining the procedure is which component of communication?
   a. Receiver
   b. Sender
   c. Listener
   d. Message

40. All of the following are used in communicating with the deaf resident EXCEPT:
   a. Pen and pad
   b. Sign language
   c. Shouting
   d. Lip reading

Answers

1. b. The Resident's Bill of Rights is a list of guidelines specifying the resident's treatment, services available, and expectations while in the health care institution.

2. c. The nurse assistant must provide the resident with privacy. The privacy rights of the resident must be adhered to during all areas of nursing care. Examples include pulling the privacy curtains during all treatments and procedures and providing appropriate clothing with buttons and zippers to prevent exposure of body parts.

3. d. The health care team members can review the health records because they all deliver care to the resident. Confidentiality is keeping the resident's medical information confidential.

4. b. The resident has the right to refuse treatment and to participate in experimental research.

5. c. The nurse assistant should encourage the resident by explaining the purpose of personal care. If the resident still refuses, the nurse assistant should report the incident to the charge nurse.

6. a. Calling the residents by their names is respectful. Using "pops," "grandpa," "sweetie," or "honey" is disrespectful. The nurse assistant is to address the resident by his or her name.

7. d. The resident is not required to deposit personal funds in the institution's account.

8. d. The resident has the right to choose his or her own personal physician. The facility must allow the residents the right to choose their own physician.

9. c. The resident has the right to voice dissatisfaction with nursing services or any facility services in the form of a grievance.

10. d. The resident has the right to have regular access to private use of the telephone.

11. d. The facility is not responsible for the stationery and postage. The residents must pay for their own stationery and stamps.

12. a. Basic needs are food, clothing, shelter, love, and security. These are necessary for day-to-day existence.

13. a. Physical needs are nutrition, personal hygiene, toileting, and dressing. These are activities of daily living (ADL) skills.

14. a. Cultural differences can be seen in a resident's preferences for food, clothing, and various lifestyles.

15. b. Each resident has a right to his or her own religious beliefs. The nurse assistant must respect each resident's beliefs and not impose their personal beliefs on the residents.

16. a. The nurse assistant must listen to what the resident is saying and understand the total complaint before it is reported to the charge nurse.

17. d. Using medical terms in communicating with the resident can cause further resident confusion. Simple questions and answers aid in effective communication.

18. d. Speech is a form of verbal communication. Nonverbal communication consists of facial expressions, gestures, body movement, and touch.

19. a. Residents with sensory impairments have a loss of vision and hearing ability. Losses of smell, speech, and taste are also sensory losses.

20. a. The ambulatory residents are evacuated first.

21. a. The nurse assistant should explain the food location on the plate, by the clock method, for blind residents.

22. d. The nurse in charge can discuss the concerns and solve the problems.

23. a. Teamwork is necessary when providing nursing care to the residents. The resident's call signal should always be answered by the first available nurse, regardless of who is assigned to that resident's care.

24. c. The nurse assistants should work together as a team and assist each other when requested.

25. a. Accept the resident and understand that the charge nurse's responsibility is to make the best decision for the resident and the staff.

26. c. The nursing assistant should take a 15-minute break in the morning, a 30-minute lunch break, and another 15-minute afternoon break. Taking breaks and lunch will decrease your body fatigue, and they are mandatory under the law.

27. c. The charge nurse has many functions and sometimes can mistakenly assign too many residents to one nurse assistant. Discuss the matter in a polite tone and allow the charge nurse the opportunity to correct the error.

28. c. The nurse assistant must promote dignity and respect during all nursing care.

29. a. Quality of life is promoting dignity and respect, allowing the resident to feel respected. Involving the resident in all phases of care is the nursing assistant's responsibility. An explanation before performing tasks is necessary.

30. a. Being polite is a form of courtesy. The nurse assistant should be kind and understanding when dealing with each resident.

31. b. Placing yourself mentally in the resident's position helps you to understand the resident's condition.

32. c. Tact is being polite, kind, and considerate at all times. Tact is used during each nursing task.

33. b. Sympathy is a feeling of sorrow for the resident or another human being.

34. b. Aggressive behavior is demanding and sometimes classified as rude.

35. d. Passive behavior is overly agreeable and quiet.

36. c. An assertive nurse can get his or her job done without being aggressive or pushy and by being firm, but not rude, during interactions with others.

37. d. Depression is a feeling of hopelessness, sadness, and low spirits. The nurse assistant will need to be supportive and understanding to residents who seem depressed.

38. a. The nonlistener is not associated with communication. A message, sender, and receiver are necessary for effective communication.

39. b. The nurse assistant is the sender of the message.

40. c. Deaf residents are unable to hear. Shouting would be an ineffective way of trying to communicate. Facing the resident allows the resident to read your lips while you speak. Offering a pencil and note pad and using sign language are additional ways to communicate with the deaf resident.

4

Medical and Legal Terminology

I. Medical Terms
    A. Word building
       1. Root
       2. Prefix
       3. Suffix

II. Vocabulary
    A. Anatomy
    B. Surgical procedures
    C. Specialty areas

III. Abbreviations
    A. Time variations
    B. Conditions
    C. Procedures

IV. Legal Responsiblity
    A. Key Terms
       1. Negligence
       2. Malpractice
       3. Invasion of privacy
       4. Assault
       5. Battery
       6. Abandonment
       7. False imprisonment
       8. Liability
       9. Ethical behavior

ABBREVIATION REFERENCE LIST

ABBREVIATION	MEANING
aa	of each, equal parts
abd.	abdomen
ABR	absolute bed rest
a.c.	before meals
A&D	admission and discharge
ad lib	as desired, if the patient so desires
ADL	activities of daily living
Adm.	admission
Adm. Spec.	admission urine specimen
A.M., a.m., am	morning
amb.	ambulation, walking, ambulatory, able to walk
amt.	amount
Approx.	approximately
aqua	water, H_2O
@	at
B&B, b&b	bowel and bladder training
bid, B.I.D., b.i.d.	twice a day
b.m., B.M.	bowel movement, feces
B.P., BP	blood pressure
BR, br, B.R., b.r.	bed rest
BRP, B.R.P., brp.	bathroom privileges
BSC, bsc	bedside commode
°C	degree Celsius (or centrigrade)
c̄	with
CA.	cancer
Cath.	catheter
CBC, C.B.C.	complete blood count
CBR, C.B.R., cbr.	complete bed rest
cc, c.c.	cubic centimeter
CCU, C.C.U.	cardiac care unit/coronary care unit
C/0, c/o	complaint of
CO_2	carbon dioxide
CS, cs, C.S., c.s.	central supply
CVA, C.V.A.	cerebrovascular accident, stroke
dc, d/c	discontinue
D.& C., D & C	dilatation and curettage
Del. Rm., d.r., DR	delivery room
Disch., D/C	discharge
DOA, D.O.A.	dead on arrival
Dr., Dr	doctor
drsg.	dressing
DX	diagnosis
E., E	enema
ECG, EKG	electrocardiogram
ED, E.D.	emergency department
EEG, E.E.G.	electroencephalogram
EENT, E.E.N.T.	eye, ears, nose, and throat
ER, E.R.	emergency room
°F	Fahrenheit degree
FBS, F.B.S.	fasting blood sugar
FF, F.F.	forced feeding, forced fluids
ft	foot
Fx	fracture
Fx urine	fractional urine
gal.	gallon
GI, G.I.	gastrointestinal
gtt.	two or more drops
GTT, G.T.T.	glucose tolerance test
GU, G.U.	genitourinary
Gyn., G.Y.N.	gynecology
H_2O	water, aqua
hr.	hour
h.s., HS, hs	bedtime, hour of sleep
ht.	height
hyper-	above or high
hypo-	below or low
H.W.B., hwb, HWB	hot water bottle
ICU, I.C.U.	intensive care unit
I & O, I. & 0.	intake and output
Irrg.	irregular
Isol., isol	isolation
IV, I.V.	intraveneous
L	liter
Lab., lab.	laboratory
lb.	pound
Liq, liq.	liquid
LPN, L.P.N.	licensed practical nurse
LVN, L.V.N.	licensed vocational nurse
M	male
Mat.	maternity
MD, M.D.	medical doctor
Meas.	measure

mec.	meconium	q.	every
med.	medicine	qam, q am, q.a.m.	every morning
min.	minute	q.d.	every day
ml.	milliliter	q.h.	every hour
Mn, mn, M/n	midnight	q. 2 h.	every 2 hours
N.A., N/A	nurse aide, nurse assistant	q. 3 h.	every 3 hours
n/g tube, ng. tube, N.G.T.	nasogastric tube	q. 4 h.	every 4 hours
Noct.	at night	Q.H.S., q.h.s.	every night at bedtime/hour of sleep
NP	neuropsychiatric, nursing procedure	q.i.d., Q.I.D.	four times a day
NPO, N.P.O.	nothing by mouth	q.o.d., Q.O.D.	every other day
N/V	nausea and vomiting	q.s.	quantity sufficient, as much as required
0²	oxygen	qt.	quart
OB, O.B.	obstetrics	r, R	rectal temperature
Obt, obt.	obtained	Rm, rm	room
OJ, O.J.	orange juice	RN, R.N.	registered nurse
OOB, O.O.B.	out of bed	rom, R.O.M.	range of motion
OPD, 0.P.D.	outpatient department	RR, R. Rm.	recovery room
OR, O.R.	operating room	Rx	prescription, treament ordered by a physician
Ord.	orderly		
Ortho.	orthopedics	s̄	without
OT, O.T.	occupational therapy, oral temperature	S&A	sugar and acetone
		S&A, S.&A. Test	sugar and acetone test
oz.	ounce	S&K, S.&K. Test	sugar and ketone test
p̄	after	SOB	shortness of breath
PAR, P.A.R.	postanesthesia room	sos.	whenever emergency arises, only if necessary
p.c.	after meals		
Ped, Peds.	pediatrics	SPD	Special Purchasing Department
per	by, through		
p.m., P.M., pm, PM	afternoon	Spec, spec.	specimen
PMC, P.M.C.	postmortem care	ss., ss	one half
PN, P.N.	pneumonia	SSE, S.S.E.	soapsuds enema
p.o.	by mouth	stat	at once, immediately
postop, post op	postoperative	Surg	surgery
post op spec	after surgery urine specimen	t.i.d., T.I.D.	three times a day
pp	postpartum (after delivery)	TLC	tender loving care
PPBS	postprandial blood sugar	TPR	temperature, pulse, respiration
pre-	before		
prn, p.r.n.	when necessary, when required	U/a, U/A, u/a	urine analysis
		ung.	ointment, unguentine
preop, pre op	before surgery	V.D., vd	veneral disease
prep	prepare the patient for surgery by shaving the skin	VDRL	test for veneral disease
		V.S., VS	vital signs
Pt, pt	patient; pint	WBC, W.B.C.	white blood count
PT, P.T.	physical therapy	w/c	wheelchair
		wt	weight

DIRECTIONS: Each question contains suggested responses. Select the one best response to each question.

ANSWERS: See answers at the end of the questions.

1. Medical terminology can be best described as:
   a. Words used by the resident
   b. Words used only by the doctors
   c. Words used only by the nurses
   d. Words used by all medical personnel

2. Which languages are primarily used in medical terminology?
   a. English and Spanish
   b. Chinese and Italian
   c. Greek and Latin
   d. German and French

3. A root word is best described as:
   a. Nucleus of the word
   b. Ending of the word
   c. Beginning of the word
   d. Beginning, middle and ending of a word

4. A prefix is included in which one of the following words?
   a. Cancer
   b. Kidney
   c. Surgery
   d. Hypertension

5. A suffix is included in which one of the following words?
   a. Respiration
   b. Extremity
   c. Cyanosis
   d. Abdominal

6. The term "anatomy" refers to:
   a. Surgical procedures
   b. Body structures
   c. Medical treatments
   d. Bodily processes

7. Physiology is best described as:
   a. Bodily functions
   b. Body structure
   c. Surgical processes
   d. Medical processes

8. The prefix cranio- refers to which part of the body?
   a. Chest
   b. Stomach
   c. Back
   d. Head

9. A prefix referring to the heart is:
   a. Cardio-
   b. Cerebro-
   c. Vertebro-
   d. Cysto-

10. Oral is best described as referring to the:
    a. Eyes
    b. Mouth
    c. Ears
    d. Arms

11. Extremities are responsible for which action?
    a. Talking
    b. Sleeping
    c. Walking
    d. Chewing

12. Gastro- is a prefix referring to which of the following body structures?
    a. Lungs
    b. Skin
    c. Teeth
    d. Stomach

13. Procto- is a prefix describing the:
    a. Rectum
    b. Intestines
    c. Uterus
    d. Liver

14. The surgical suffix -otomy refers to a:
    a. Surgical incision
    b. Surgical removal
    c. Surgical opening
    d. Surgical adduction

15. The surgical suffix -ectomy best describes a:
    a. Surgical opening
    b. Surgical incision
    c. Surgical removal
    d. Surgical reduction

16. The surgical suffix -ostomy refers to a:
    a. Surgical adduction
    b. Surgical opening
    c. Surgical incision
    d. Surgical removal

17. All of the following statements are *true* regarding specialty areas EXCEPT:
    a. Specific conditions are treated
    b. Specialists treat the condition or disease
    c. Subspecialties are more specific
    d. Treatment is nonspecific

18. A short version of a medical term is best described as:
    a. Prefix
    b. Suffix
    c. Abbreviation
    d. Word root

19. The standard abbreviation "q" refers to:
    a. Every
    b. Daily
    c. Nightly
    d. Sometimes

20. Select appropriate abbreviation for "every morning."
    a. q P.M.
    b. q a.m.
    c. q. H.S.
    d. q Noc

21. How often should the resident be repositioned?
    a. q h.
    b. q. 2 h.
    c. q. 3 h.
    d. q. 4 h.

22. The nurse assistant can best describe B.i.d. as:
    a. Three times a day
    b. Four times a day
    c. Twice a day
    d. Once a day

23. Three times a day is best described as:
    a. bid
    b. t.i.d.
    c. q.i.d.
    d. q. 3 h.

24. Four times a day is best described as:
    a. q.i.d.
    b. t.i.d.
    c. q. 4 h.
    d. bid

25. The acronym CA. refers to which of the following?
    a. Chance
    b. Cancer
    c. Catheter
    d. Cardiac

26. The abbreviation CVA refers to:
    a. Cardiovascular system
    b. Congestive heart failure
    c. Cerebral vascular accident
    d. Cardiac arrest

27. Select the appropriate abbreviation for hypertension.
    a. HTN
    b. HPN
    c. HYP
    d. HYTN

28. An infection in the urinary system is best described by which abbreviation?
    a. UTI
    b. URT
    c. URI
    d. USI

29. Which abbreviation best describes nothing by mouth?
    a. NBO
    b. NPO
    c. NOP
    d. NBM

30. SSE is best described as a:
    a. Treatment for constipation
    b. Treatment for flatus
    c. Treatment for seizures
    d. Treatment for diabetes

31. All of the following foods should be calculated for intake and output (I & 0) EXCEPT:
   a. Juice
   b. Ice cream
   c. Water
   d. Pudding

32. Failure to raise the resident's side rail is an example of:
   a. Negligence
   b. Malpractice
   c. Accident
   d. Incident

33. The doctor prescribing an incorrect medication for the resident is an example of:
   a. Malpractice
   b. Negligence
   c. Assault
   d. Battery

34. Exposing the resident's body unnecessarily is an example of:
   a. Battery
   b. Privacy invasion
   c. Criminal law
   d. Libel

35. Verbally threatening to cause the resident bodily harm is best described as:
   a. Slander
   b. Battery
   c. Assault
   d. Libel

36. Twisting the resident's arm to encourage cooperation during a task is best described as:
   a. Battery
   b. Slander
   c. Libel
   d. Assault

37. Select the term that should be used to describe resident neglect.
   a. False imprisonment
   b. Defamation
   c. Abandonment
   d. Slander

38. Select the term that best describes restraining a resident without a written order.
   a. Libel
   b. Abandonment
   c. Slander
   d. False imprisonment

39. Select the term that defines liability.
   a. An obligation incurred or that might be incurred through any act or failure to act
   b. A violation against a citizen of society
   c. An assault that is actually carried out when a person is injured
   d. An unsuccessful attempt or threat to commit bodily harm

40. Ethical behavior is best described as all of the following EXCEPT:
   a. Untrustworthy
   b. Confidentiality
   c. Dependability
   d. Accuracy

Answers

1. d.   Medical terminology consists of medical terms used by medically trained personnel.

2. c.   Greek and Latin words are primarily used in medical terminology. For example, in "sphygmomanometer" *sphygmo* is the pulse; *mano* is the pressure; *meter* is the measurement.

3. a.   The root word is the nucleus of the word.

4. d.   Prefixes add to or subtract from the root word. The prefix changes the meaning of the root word. Examples are *hyper*tension and *hypo*tension.

5. c.   Cyanosis has a suffix, *osis*, which is a disease condition of the root word. For example, in pancrea*titis*, *itis* is the inflammation of the root word.

6. b.   The structure of the body is called its anatomy.

7. a.   Physiology is the sutdy of bodily function.

8. d.   The prefix cranio- refers to the head or skull.

9. a. The prefix cardio- refers to the heart.

10. b. The term oral refers to the mouth.

11. c. The term extremities refers to the arms and legs.

12. d. The prefix gastro- refers to the stomach.

13. a. The prefix procto- refers to the rectum.

14. a. The suffix -otomy refers to a surgical incision.

15. c. The suffix -ectomy refers to the surgical removal of an organ.

16. b. The suffix -ostomy refers to a surgical opening.

17. d. Specialty areas treat each area of the body separately and are specific. There is a specialist, a physician, who has studied in depth the specific condition and treatment plan.

18. c. Abbreviation is writing the short form of a medical term. For example, nurse assistant is abbreviated as N.A.; certified nursing assistant is C.N.A.

19. a. Every is abbreviated q. For example, every morning is abbreviated as q a.m.

20. b. Every morning is abbreviated q a.m.

21. b. The resident should be turned every 2 hours (q 2h.).

22. c. The time frame b.i.d. is twice a day.

23. b. Three times a day is t.i.d.

24. a. The time frame is q.i.d.

25. b. CA refers to cancer.

26. c. A cerebrovascular accident is a stroke, abbreviated as CVA.

27. a. HTN is the abbreviation for hypertension.

28. a. UTI is the abbreviation for urinary tract infection.

29. b. NPO is nothing by mouth.

30. a. SSE is a soap suds enema given to treat constipation.

31. d. Puddings are a solid food source and would not be calculated on I & 0. Liquids taken into the resident's body and fluids discharged from resident's body are calculated on intake and output.

32. a. Negligence is the failure to perform properly a task in your job specification.

33. a. Malpractice is bad practice by a professional.

34. b. Failure to prevent unnecessary exposure of the body during a task is invasion of the resident's privacy.

35. c. Verbal threats of injury constitute assault.

36. a. Causing bodily harm to the resident is battery.

37. c. Failure to provide nursing care to a resident assigned to your care is called abandonment.

38. d. Restraining a resident without a doctor's order is a form of false imprisonment.

39. a. A liability is an obligation incurred or that might be incurred by an act or failure to act.

40. a. Untrustworthiness is not a part of ethical behavior. Confidentiality, dependability, and accuracy are key areas of ethical behavior.

5

Personal Care and Elimination Needs

DIRECTIONS: Each question contains suggested responses. Select the one best response to each question.

ANSWERS: See answers at the end of the questions.

1. Personal hygiene is best described as all of the following EXCEPT:
   a. Mouth care
   b. Bathing
   c. Nail care
   d. Vital signs

2. Select the appropriate personal care before bedtime.
   a. A.M. care
   b. H.S. care
   c. B.T. care
   d. P.M. care

3. Oral hygiene is best described as:
   a. Mouth care
   b. Face care
   c. Hair care
   d. Nail care

4. Select the appropriate head position for mouth care to the unconscious resident.
   a. Toward the nurse
   b. Away from the nurse
   c. Straight forward
   d. Hyperextended

5. Which one of the following items is used to give mouth care to the unconscious resident?
   a. Toothbrush
   b. Toothpaste
   c. Glycerine swabs
   d. Gargle solution

6. All of the following directions are appropriate to brush the conscious resident's teeth EXCEPT:
   a. Side-to-side motion
   b. Upward motion
   c. Downward motion
   d. Circular motion

7. Select the appropriate mouthwash dilution:
   a. One-fourth water
   b. One-half water
   c. Three-fourths water
   d. No water necessary

8. Which one of the following is the correct method of removing upper dentures?
   a. Pull dentures straight out
   b. Pull up on the dentures
   c. Gently push down on the dentures
   d. Move the dentures side to side

9. All of the following are true regarding dentures EXCEPT:
   a. Removed at night
   b. Brushed after each meal
   c. Must be kept moist
   d. Stored in hot water

10. Which type of resident is given a complete bed bath?
    a. Weak
    b. Ambulatory
    c. Confused
    d. Deaf

11. All of the following equipment is necessary for a bed bath EXCEPT:
    a. Wash basin
    b. Towels
    c. Bath blanket
    d. Bath mat

12. Select appropriate water temperature for a tub bath.
    a. 105°F
    b. 110°F
    c. 115°F
    d. 120°F

13. Which part of the body is washed first during the bath?
    a. Neck
    b. Chest
    c. Arms
    d. Face

14. During a tub bath the nurse assistant should do all of the following EXCEPT:
    a. Place a towel inside the tub

b. Place a towel outside the tub

c. Leave the resident unattended

d. Fill the tub half full

15. A shower is given to which type of resident?
    a. Extremely weak
    b. Wheelchair dependent
    c. Nonambulatory
    d. Ambulatory

16. All of the following are observations to be made during oral hygiene EXCEPT:
    a. Odor
    b. Decubitus
    c. Lip cracks
    d. Sores

17. The purposes of a bath are all of the following EXCEPT:
    a. Increase skin dryness
    b. Promote relaxation
    c. Increase circulation
    d. Promote hygiene

18. Shaving is provided how often?
    a. Every day
    b. Every other day
    c. Once a week
    d. As needed

19. All of the following are abnormal observations after hair care EXCEPT:
    a. Sores
    b. Healthy hair
    c. Hair lice
    d. Excessive dandruff

20. Which statement is true regarding nail care?
    a. Nails are trimmed straight across.
    b. Nails are trimmed in a V shape.
    c. Nails are to be kept long.
    d. Nails are soaked after trimming.

21. The purposes of skin care are best described as all of the following except:
    a. Restores skin oils
    b. Promotes circulation
    c. Observation is not necessary
    d. Prevents skin breakdown

22. The affected portion of the body is dressed first in which type of resident?
    a. Hard of hearing
    b. Confused
    c. Paralyzed
    d. Blind

23. Which systems are involved in elimination?
    a. Circulatory and skeletal
    b. Reproductive and endocrine
    c. Nervous and respiratory
    d. Gastrointestinal and excretory

24. Select the system which breaks down food
    a. Gastrointestinal
    b. Respiratory
    c. Circulatory
    d. Integumentary System

25. All of the following refer to elimination EXCEPT:
    a. Stool
    b. Feces
    c. Urine
    d. Emesis

26. Which system is responsible for the formation of urine?
    a. Reproductive
    b. Digestive
    c. Excretory
    d. Endocrine

27. Which one of the following is the end product of digestion?
    a. Food
    b. Feces
    c. Nutrition
    d. Dehydration

28. Perineal care is best described as all of the following EXCEPT:
    a. Washing the vaginal area
    b. Washing the rectal area
    c. Washing the scrotal area
    d. Washing the axillary area

29. A stage 2 decubitus is best described as:
    a. Redden area
    b. Open redden area

c. Exposed muscle

d. Exposed bone

30. The resident is unable to defecate. Select the appropriate term.
    a. Constipation
    b. Diarrhea
    c. Flatus
    d. Nausea

31. Defecation is best described as:
    a. Nausea and vomiting
    b. Bowel movement
    c. Urination
    d. Perspiration

32. Diarrhea is best described as frequent:
    a. Watery stool
    b. Soft stool
    c. Loose stool
    d. Hard stool

33. All of the following statements are true regarding enemas EXCEPT:
    a. A liquid placed in the rectum
    b. Requires a physcian's order
    c. Requires nurse assistant permission
    d. Relieves constipation

34. A Harris flush relieves which one of the following?
    a. Flatus
    b. Diarrhea
    c. Itching
    d. Weakness

35. Select the appropriate term for flatus.
    a. Urine
    b. Gas

c. Stool

d. Perspiration

36. Which one of the following foods can increase intestinal gas formation?
    a. Onions
    b. Jell-o
    c. Fruit
    d. Pudding

37. A protrusion of the abdomen is best described as:
    a. Extension
    b. Friction
    c. Flexion
    d. Distention

38. Lack of control of the bowel and bladder is best described as:
    a. Continence
    b. Incontinence
    c. Constipation
    d. Diarrhea

39. All of the following are used in elimination EXCEPT:
    a. Emesis basis
    b. Commode
    c. Urinal
    d. Bedpan

40. All of the following nursing measures will prevent skin irritations EXCEPT:
    a. Removing urine and stool immediately
    b. Repositioning every three hours
    c. Washing, rinsing, and drying the skin
    d. Using lotions to protect the skin

Answers

1. d. Vital signs are not a part of personal hygiene.

2. b. H.S. care is done before bedtime and includes washing the face and hands and mouth care. The nurse assistant would also give a backrub.

3. a. Oral hygiene is mouth care.

4. a. The proper head position is toward the nurse. Placing the resident's head to the side facing the nurse will allow visualization of the mouth and prevent aspiration.

5. c. Glycerine swabs are used to clean the mouth of the unconscious resident.

6. d. The teeth are to be brushed upward and downward, as well as from side to side.

7. b. One-half water with one-half mouthwash is appropriate.

8. c. The upper dentures are removed by gently pushing downward.

9. d. Dentures are never stored in hot water. The hot water may alter the shape of the dentures.

10. a. Residents who are on bedrest or whose condition is too critical to transfer are given a bed bath.

11. d. A bath mat is only necessary when you are giving a tub bath.

12. a. 105°F is the correct water temperature. A bath thermometer can validate the correct temperature of water.

13. d. The face is washed first.

14. c. The resident should be supervised closely to prevent accidents.

15. d. A shower is given to the stronger and ambulatory resident.

16. b. The mouth is observed for cracks, sores, and odors.

17. a. The purpose of a bath is to increase circulation, promote relaxation, and promote hygiene.

18. d. Hair growth may vary from resident to resident. Shave the resident as often as needed.

19. b. Healthy hair is not abnormal. Report problems such as sores, hair lice, hair loss, and excessive dandruff.

20. a. The nails are to be cut straight across.

21. c. Observation is very important during skin care. Any abnormalities such as redden areas or open areas must be reported.

22. c. The paralyzed resident must have the affected side dressed first.

23. d. The gastrointestinal and excretory systems are necessary for elimination.

24. a. The gastrointestinal system breaks down food for the body to metabolize.

25. d. Elimination is discharging waste from the body in the form of urine or stool.

26. c. The excretory or urinary system is responsible for the formation of urine.

27. b. The end product of digestion is feces; other names are stool, bowel movement, or fecal matter.

28. d. The axillary area is the armpit. This is not part of perineal care.

29. b. A stage 2 decubitus is an open redden area.

30. a. Constipation is inability or difficulty in passing stool.

31. b. Defecation is passing stool or a bowel movement.

32. a. Diarrhea is frequent watery stools.

33. c. The nurse assistant's permission is not the deciding factor. The physician gives the order and the charge nurse gives permission to the nurse assistant.

34. a. A Harris flush relieves flatus.

35. b. Flatus is the medical term for intestinal gas.

36. a. Onions can increase gas formation.

37. d. Distention is the protrusion of the abdomen.

38. b. Incontinence is lack of control of the bowels or bladder.

39. a. The emesis basin is not an elimination item. Elimination items are the bedpan, urinal, and bedside commode.

40. b. The residents must be repositioned every 2 hours.

6

Resident Safety and Infection Control

QUESTIONS

DIRECTIONS: Each question contains four suggested responses. Select the one best response to each question.

ANSWERS: See answers at the end of the questions.

1. Select the first action by the nurse assistant before performing a nursing procedure.
   a. Explain the procedure
   b. Check the armband
   c. Provide privacy
   d. Lower the siderail

2. All of the following will prevent falls EXCEPT:
   a. Dangling before transfer
   b. Securing the siderails
   b. Locking the wheelchair
   d. Spills on the floor

3. Dangling is best described as:
   a. Sitting the resident on the side of the bed
   b. Standing the resident on the side of the bed
   c. Lifting the resident to the wheelchair
   d. Pushing the resident in the wheelchair

4. The resident is to be transferred to the wheelchair. Select the appropriate action of the nurse assistant.
   a. Lock the wheelchair after the transfer
   b. Lock the wheelchair during the transfer
   c. Lock the wheelchair before the transfer
   d. Locking the wheelchair is not necessary

5. Which action should the nurse assistant take to prevent a collision in a blind corridor?
   a. Proceed at full speed
   b. Slow your speed until clearance is complete
   c. Stop, check both ways, and then proceed
   d. Stopping is not necessary since wheelchairs have the right of way

6. Which muscles are used most often in body mechanics?
   a. Back muscles
   b. Arm muscles
   c. Neck muscles
   d. Thigh muscles

7. Which statement is true regarding the wearing of rubber-soled shoes in the health care facility?
   a. Decreases the risk of slipping
   b. Increases the risk of accidents
   c. Allows greater mobility
   d. Stabilizes the foot

8. STAT is described best as:
   a. Immediately
   b. Later
   c. Eventually
   d. Maybe

9. Which action defines the nurse assistant's response to a STAT page?
   a. Walk slowly to area paged
   b. Run as fast as you can
   c. Arrive 10 minutes after the page
   d. Walk rapidly, do not run

10. Select the appropriate safety precaution after performing a nursing task.
    a. Open the privacy curtain
    b. Specify the next room visit
    c. Place the call signal in reach
    d. Position the resident on the right side

11. Which one of the following is a standard nursing precaution for the bed-bound resident?
    a. Fowler's bed position at all times
    b. Siderails up at all times
    c. Siderails released
    d. Siderails lowered at the resident's request

12. All of the following are safety precautions during a tub bath EXCEPT:
    a. Placing a towel outside the tub
    b. Leaving the resident alone during the tub bath
    c. Placing a towel inside the tub
    d. Using a soap dispenser

13. Having a broad base of support with the feet 12 inches apart would best describe the action in which nursing skill?
    a. Feeding
    b. Handwashing
    c. Positioning
    d. Documentation

14. All of the following are safety precautions in regard to infant care EXCEPT:
    a. Crib siderails up at all times
    b. No plastics left near the infant
    c. Supervise closely
    d. Propping feeding bottle for convenience

15. All of the following are oxygen therapy precautions EXCEPT:
    a. Removing electrical appliances
    b. Monitoring the amount of oxygen in the tank
    c. Checking the oxygen tubing for kinks
    d. Allowing the resident to smoke

16. Safety precautions when using electrical appliances include all of the following except:
    a. Inserting plugs with wet hands
    b. Monitoring the floor for spills
    c. Never overloading the circuits
    d. Replacing defective appliances

17. Ambulation safety is best described as:
    a. Using a gait belt to prevent falling
    b. Supporting to prevent slipping
    c. Walking in front of the resident
    d. Walking behind the resident

18. Fire safety is best described as all of the following EXCEPT:
    a. Teaching the resident safety precautions
    b. Frequent fire drills
    c. Regular service checks on various extinguishers
    d. Defective fire alarms

19. Which procedure is used for the silent chocking victim?
    a. Blows to the back
    b. Raising the arms upward
    c. Heimlich maneuver
    d. CPR

20. Protective devices are best described as:
    a. Restraints
    b. Dressings
    c. Call signals
    d. Privacy curtains

21. A nurse assistant finds the resident unconscious in bed. Select the first response.
    a. Turn on the call signal
    b. Check for breathing
    c. Start CPR
    d. Check for pulse

22. Hemorrhage is excessive bleeding. Select the appropriate treatment.
    a. Heat to the area
    b. Pressure to the area
    c. Movement of the area
    d. Downward position

23. All of the following are emergency treatments for burns EXCEPT:
    a. Cold water
    b. Sterile dressings
    c. Pressure
    d. Ice pack

24. During a seizure the nurse assistant should understand all of the following EXCEPT:
    a. Restraining the resident is necessary.
    b. Head position is to the side.
    c. Sleeping may occur after the seizure.
    d. Sharp areas of furniture must be padded.

25. All of the following are actions of the nurse assistant during a suspected heart attack occurring inside the resident's room EXCEPT:
    a. Checking for breathing
    b. Checking for circulation
    c. Checking for response
    d. Leaving to get help

26. All of the following are poison precautions EXCEPT:
    a. Nonlabeled bottles
    b. Separating internal and external medication
    c. Good observations
    d. Poisons kept in a locked cabinet

27. The Heimlich maneuver is best described as:
    a. Pressure to the upper abdomen
    b. Pressure to the sternum
    c. A finger sweep
    d. Raising the arms in the upward direction

28. Select the first action of the nurse assistant before applying a restraint.
    a. Ask a coworker to assist
    b. Pull the privacy curtain
    c. Explain the procedure
    d. Check for the physician's order

29. Restraints are released how often?
    a. Every hour
    b. Every 2 hours
    c. Every 3 hours
    d. Every 4 hours

30. Microorganisms are best described as all of the following EXCEPT:
    a. Tiny organisms
    b. Can only be seen with a microscope
    c. Can be seen without a microscope
    d. Harmful and harmless

31. A germ can cause which one of the following conditions?
    a. Seizure
    b. Infection
    c. Stroke
    d. Diabetes

32. All of the following are signs of infection EXCEPT:
    a. Redness
    b. Fever
    c. Pain
    d. Cyanosis

33. Examples of contagious diseases are all of the following EXCEPT:
    a. Tuberculosis
    b. Scabies
    c. Measles
    d. Diabetes

34. Which one of the following can destroy all bacteria?
    a. Darkness
    b. Sunlight

c. Moisture
d. Autoclave

35. Which statement is true regarding the autoclave?
    a. Destroys three fourths of the germs on an object
    b. Destroys one-half of the germs on an object
    c. Destroys one-fourth of the germs on an object
    d. Destroys all germs on an object

36. Universal precautions are designed to protect health care workers from which diseases?
    a. Strokes and seizures
    b. Contractures and paralysis
    c. AIDS and hepatitis
    d. Diabetes and hypertension

37. The purposes of isolation technique are all of the following EXCEPT:
    a. Protection of the resident
    b. Allowing germs to leave the room
    c. Protection of the employee
    d. Protection of the visitor

38. The resident in isolation should have all of the following EXCEPT:
    a. Visible door sign of the type of isolation
    b. Visible door signs of the isolation dress code
    c. Nondisposable eating utensils
    d. Stocked isolation cart outside the room

39. Select the appropriate disposal method of isolation contaminated articles.
    a. Use one bag and close tightly
    b. Place in regular linen hamper
    c. Use two bags inside the room
    d. Use one bag in the room; place it in a second bag outside the room

40. Which statement is true regarding the removal of gown, mask, and gloves?
    a. Remove gloves and gown, wash hands, remove mask, and wash hands
    b. Remove gown, wash hands, and remove gloves and mask
    c. Remove mask, wash hands, and remove gown and gloves
    d. Remove any of the items first; it doesn't matter

Answers

1. b. Checking the armband ensures the correct resident for the procedure.

2. d. Removing spills promptly from the floor will prevent falls.

3. a. Dangling is sitting the resident on the side of the bed. This gives the nurse assistant the opportunity to check the resident for dizziness or extreme weakness.

4. c. The wheelchair is locked before the transfer to prevent the chair from moving.

5. c. Stop and look both ways. If there is no traffic, proceed.

6. d. The thigh muscles are used most often in body mechanics. These are stronger and larger muscles. The back is kept straight, saving the back muscles from injury.

7. a. Rubber-soled shoes grip the floor and aid in preventing accidents.

8. a. STAT is a medical term meaning immediately.

9. d. Walking rapidly, but not running, can prevent a collision.

10. c. Placing the call signal in reach is a safety precaution.

11. b. Siderails are kept up at all times. The resident should have a siderail release in the front of the chart, if the rail is to be left down. This is a safety precaution.

12. b. To prevent any accidents in the tub, the resident should not be left unattended.

13. c. A broad base of support with feet 12 inches apart is used in positioning the resident.

14. d. Propping the infant's feeding bottle for convenience can result in choking of the infant.

15. d. An oxygen precaution is NO SMOKING.

16. a. Never use wet hands to insert plugs. This can cause an electrical burn or shock.

17. a. To prevent falls during ambulation, use a gait belt to support the resident.

18. d. A defective fire alarm is unsafe in case of fire.

19. c. The Heimlich maneuver is applying pressure to the midsection to dislodge a food obstruction in the throat.

20. a. A protective device is a restraint. Occasionally, residents are restrained to prevent injury to themselves and others.

21. a. Calling for help first and staying with the unconscious resident will enable the nurse assistant to open the airway or start CPR, if necessary.

22. b. To stop bleeding, pressure is applied above or directly to the bleeding area.

23. c. Emergency treatment for burns is cold water, ice packs, and sterile dressings. Pressure is not a treatment for burns.

24. a. Restraining the resident is not necessary. Provide a safe environment; i.e., move any furniture or unsafe objects out of the way during the seizure. Position the resident's head to the side to prevent aspirating or choking.

25. d. During a suspected heart attack the nurse assistant should not leave the resident unattended.

26. a. A poison precaution is making sure all medications are in labeled bottles.

27. a. The Heimlich maneuver is holding the resident around the upper waist area, with the hand next to the abdomen in a fist form, and applying pressure. The above will help to dislodge an obstruction in the throat area.

28. d. Restraints must have a physician's order before for application.

29. b. The resident must be checked at least every 30 minutes for adequate circulation and released every 2 hours.

30. c. Microorganisms cannot be seen without a microscope.

31. b. Germs can cause infections.

32. d. Cyanosis is a sign of lack of oxygen, in which the skin turns blue. Redness, fever, and pain are some signs of infection.

33. d. A contagious disease is easily transferred from person to person through touching and breathing.

34. d. The autoclave destroys all bacteria.

35. d. The autoclave removes all germs, leaving the object sterile.

36. c. AIDS and hepatitis residents are at high risk for transferring their diseases to the health care worker. Blood and body fluids are highly contagious and universal precautions must be followed.

37. b. The purpose of isolation techniques is to keep the germs isolated to the room and keep the resident from contracting other germs in the facility.

38. c. The resident in isolation should have disposable eating utensils to decrease the opportunity of germs leaving the isolation unit.

39. d. The articles inside the room are bagged. A coworker stands outside the door with an open bag to double bag articles.

40. a. Removal of isolation garments such as gloves, mask, and gown are done in the following manner: gloves and gown are removed first, hands are washed, the mask is removed, and hands are washed again.

7

Bedmaking, Body Mechanics, and Positioning

QUESTIONS

DIRECTIONS: Each question contains four suggested responses. Select the one best response to each question.

ANSWERS: See answers at the end of the questions.

1. Lowering the bed to a comfortable position will prevent:
   a. Back strain
   b. Arm strain
   c. Neck strain
   d. Leg strain

2. Body mechanics is best described as:
   a. Infection prevention
   b. Prevention of body fatigue and injury
   c. A surgical procedure
   d. Frequent use of back muscles

3. All of the following are true regarding bed cranks EXCEPT:
   a. Can raise and lower the bed
   b. Can cause leg injuries
   c. Are left extended from the bed
   d. Must be replaced after use

4. The purpose of making one side of the bed at a time is:
   a. To prevent fatigue
   b. To increase circulation
   c. To exercise body parts
   d. To increase fatigue

5. Which statement is true regarding worn or torn linen?
   a. Fold away from the resident's body
   b. Can be used but must be reported to the charge nurse
   c. Should not be used
   d. Can be used for cleaning the furniture

6. Select the appropriate safety precaution to prevent damage to the linen and mattress.
   a. Attaching the call signal with a safety pin
   b. Using metal clamps to attach the call signal
   c. Allowing the call signal to hang behind the bed
   d. Taping the call signal to the resident's clothing

7. Select the appropriate method of handling linen during bedmaking.
   a. Shake vigorously
   b. Unfold on the bed
   c. Unfold in the linen room
   d. Allow contact with the floor

8. The nurse assistant should hold the linen in which position?
   a. Away from the uniform
   b. Next to the uniform
   c. Directly under the arm
   d. To the right of the body

9. Shaking the linen is a violation of which of the following principles.
   a. Safety
   b. Infection control
   c. Dignity
   d. Independence

10. Select the appropriate action if the sheet touches the floor during bedmaking.
    a. Continue to make the bed
    b. Place the contaminated part away from the resident
    c. Replace the sheet
    d. Report the incident to the charge nurse

11. A wrinkle-free bed will prevent which of the following conditions?
    a. Decubitus
    b. Rash
    c. Abrasion
    d. Punctures

12. Which of the following actions will prevent linen waste?
    a. Taking two of each piece of linen into the room
    b. Taking the exact amount of linen needed into the room
    c. Estimating the amount of linen needed
    d. Linen waste is not important

13. Select the appropriate action of the nurse assistant regarding extra linen in the unit.
    a. Use only in that unit.
    b. Replace in the linen closet.

c. Place on your linen cart.

d. Give to your coworker.

14. All of the following statements are true regarding linen hampers EXCEPT:

a. Used to store dirty linen

b. Must be covered at all times

c. Must be separated from clean linen cart

d. Can be left uncovered

15. All of the following statements are true regarding dirty linen EXCEPT:

a. Is carried away from your uniform

b. Cannot be placed at the foot of the bed for a short period

c. Can be placed on the floor for a short period

d. Is placed in a covered hamper

16. An open bed is best described as:

a. Without covers

b. Assigned to a resident

c. Ready for an admission

d. Without side rails

17. Which type of bed is clean and ready for an admission?

a. Open

b. Occupied

c. Closed

d. Postoperative

18. All of the following types of residents can be out of the bed for bedmaking EXCEPT:

a. Confused

b. Nonambulatory

c. Ambulatory

d. Bed rest

19. All of the following refer to the postoperative bed EXCEPT:

a. Closed

b. O.R.

c. Recovery

d. Surgical

20. A postoperative bed is made with the covers in which direction?

a. Folded to the top of the bed

b. No folds are necessary

c. Folded to one side of the bed

d. Folded to the middle of the bed

21. The purpose of the postoperative bed is which of the following?

a. Allows easier entry after surgery

b. Saves time and energy

c. Allows easier transfer before the surgery

d. Allows the resident to assist during the transfer

22. All of the following are parts of the bed EXCEPT:

a. Cranks

b. Controls

c. Side rails

d. Foot stool

23. An air mattress prevents which of the following?

a. Rashes

b. Decubitus

c. Seizures

d. Contracture

24. An egg crate mattress is best described as a:

a. Foam cushion

b. Air cushion

c. Water cushion

d. Sand cushion

25. A footboard prevents which of the following?

a. Foot rash

b. Foot ulcer

c. Foot drop

d. Foot odor

26. A bed cradle prevents which of the following?

a. Mattress sliding

b. Covers from touching the resident

c. Contracture of the body

d. Pressure on the back

27. A kick pleat is best described as:

a. Toe space

b. A mitered corner

c. A triangular corner

d. A mitten

28. Select the appropriate diagnosis for waterbed therapy:
    a. Seizures
    b. Comatose
    c. Dehydrated
    d. Thick skin

29. A call signal is not working properly. Select the appropriate response.
    a. Check the resident every hour.
    b. Report to the charge nurse immediately.
    c. Have the resident use roommate's signal.
    d. Give the resident a whistle to blow.

30. The hospital unit must have all of the following EXCEPT:
    a. Privacy curtain
    b. Closets
    c. Bedside table
    d. Nonworking call signal

31. Body mechanics is used most frequently during:
    a. Feeding
    b. Bathing
    c. Transferring
    d. Charting

32. All of the following are rules for lifting EXCEPT:
    a. Keep your back straight.
    b. Hold the object close to your body.
    c. Bend from the waist.
    d. Use leg muscles.

33. Good posture during a resident's transfer is which of the following?
    a. Body aligned, knees bent and body balanced
    b. Knees straight, back bent
    c. Feet together, knees straight
    d. Twist your body, work against the gravity

34. A supine position is best described as:
    a. Lying on your right side
    b. Lying on your stomach
    c. Lying on your back
    d. Lying on your left side

35. The Fowler's position is best described as:
    a. Sitting in bed at a 45° to 90° angle
    b. Flat in bed
    c. Lying on a side
    d. Lying face down

36. Prone position is best described as:
    a. Lying on the back
    b. Lying face down
    c. Lying on a side
    d. Sitting on the side of the bed

37. Select the appropriate position for an enema:
    a. Prone
    b. Supine
    c. Sim's
    d. Fowler's

38. Dangling is best described as:
    a. Sitting on the side of the bed
    b. Sitting up in bed
    c. Lying in bed
    d. Standing at the foot of the bed

39. Select the appropriate method of moving the resident to the side of the bed.
    a. Assist the resident into a dangling position.
    b. Use the log roll to the right side.
    c. Use the draw sheet to turn the resident to the side.
    d. Move head, body and legs in sections.

40. The purpose of repositioning every 2 hours is all of the following EXCEPT:
    a. Decrease circulation
    b. Prevent decubitus
    c. Prevent prolonged pressure
    d. Promote circulation

Answers

1. a. Lowering the bed to a comfortable position will prevent excessive strain on the back muscles.

2. b. Body mechanics is moving the body to prevent fatigue.

3. c. Bed cranks should be replaced after each use.

4. a. Making one side of the bed at a time will conserve energy and decrease fatigue.

5. c. As a safety precaution, worn and torn linen should not be used.

6. b. Metal clamps will not puncture or damage the linen or mattress. Never use safety pins on the linen or mattress.

7. b. The linen is unfolded on the bed during bedmaking. Shaking the linen spreads germs.

8. a. Clean and dirty linen is held away from the uniform.

9. b. Shaking the linen spreads germs through the room. This is a violation of infection control precautions.

10. c. The sheet is classified as contaminated or dirty and must be replaced.

11. a. A wrinkle-free bed will prevent decubitus.

12. b. Taking the exact amount of linen into the room will prevent linen abuse.

13. a. Extra linen in the unit can only be used in that unit. Never return it to the linen closet because of the germs in the unit.

14. d. The linen hampers must be covered at all times to decrease odors and promote infection control.

15. c. Dirty linen must be placed in the linen hamper, never on the floor, to promote infection control.

16. b. An open bed is already assigned to a resident.

17. c. The closed bed is clean and ready for an admission.

18. d. An occupied bed is made for a resident on bed rest.

19. a. A postoperative bed is an O.R. bed, a recovery bed, and a surgical bed. A closed bed is not associated with a postoperative bed.

20. c. The covers on a postoperative bed are folded to the right or left side of the bed, depending on the location of the door.

21. a. The purpose of a postoperative bed is to allow easy entry after the surgery.

22. d. The foot stool is separate from the bed and is used as a safety aid when stepping from the bed.

23. b. An air mattress will aid in the prevention of decubitus.

24. a. An egg crate mattress is a foam pad, resembling the bottom of an egg carton, which is used to decrease pressure.

25. c. A footboard prevents foot drop by keeping the foot in an upright position.

26. b. A bed cradle prevents covers from touching the body.

27. a. A kick pleat is a fold in the foot of the covers allowing extra room for the feet.

28. b. Comatose resident require frequent positioning and skin care to prevent decubitus. A water mattress will prevent pressure on bony areas.

29. b. Report the nonworking call signal to the charge nurse for repairs.

30. d. The call signal must be working at all times. The resident may have an emergency and need the nurse assistant immediately.

31. c. Body mechanics is used most frequently during transferring.

32. c. The rules for lifting include stooping, never bending from the waist. Keep your back straight, hold the object close to your body, and use your upper leg muscles.

33. a. Good posture during a transfer is body aligned, knees bent, and a broad base of support which balances the body.

34. c. A supine position is lying on your back.

35. a. A Fowler's position is sitting up in bed at a 45° to 90° angle.

36. b. The prone position is lying face down.

37. c. A Sim's position is lying on the right or left side.

38. a. Dangling is sitting on the side of the bed.

39. d. Moving the resident to the side of the bed is done in sections—head, body, and legs.

40. a. Repositioning every 2 hours promotes circulation, prevents prolonged pressure to an area and prevents decubitus. Turning every 2 hours increases circulation.

8

Nutrition, Diets, and Feeding Techniques

DIRECTIONS: Each question contains four suggested responses. Select the one best response to each question.

ANSWERS: See answers at the end of the questions.

1. The body's process of using food is best described as:
   a. Elimination
   b. Nutrition
   c. Digestion
   d. Peristalsis

2. Which of the following is a chemical substance found in food?
   a. Calorie
   b. Pounds
   c. Nutrient
   d. Cell

3. An individual specializing in residents' meal preparation is a:
   a. Dietitian
   b. Physician
   c. Nurse practitioner
   d. Nutritionist

4. Select the appropriate number of nutrients necessary to help build the body.
   a. 25
   b. 35
   c. 40
   d. 50

5. All of the following are necessary in nutrient formation EXCEPT:
   a. Soil
   b. Darkness
   c. Sun
   d. Water

6. All of the following are examples of nutrients EXCEPT:
   a. Proteins
   b. Carbohydrates
   c. Alcohol
   d. Vitamins

7. Select the appropriate nutrient necessary for work energy and body temperature.
   a. Protein
   b. Carbohydrates
   c. Minerals
   d. Vitamins

8. Which nutrient builds and renews body tissue?
   a. Minerals
   b. Fats
   c. Vitamins
   d. Proteins

9. Which nutrient is the carrier of vitamins A and D?
   a. Fats
   b. Proteins
   c. Water
   d. Carbohydrates

10. Select the appropriate nutrient which regulates body processes.
    a. Proteins
    b. Water
    c. Minerals
    d. Vitamins

11. Select the appropriate nutrient which builds and renews bones and teeth.
    a. Water
    b. Carbohydrates
    c. Proteins
    d. Minerals

12. Select the appropriate nutrient which prevents night blindness.
    a. Minerals
    b. Proteins
    c. Vitamins
    d. Carbohydrates

13. A balanced diet consists of foods from which one of the following groups?
    a. Three basic food groups
    b. Food guide pyramid
    c. Four basic food groups
    d. Six basic food groups

14. All of the following are foods from the food guide pyramid EXCEPT:
    a. Bread and cereal
    b. Vegetable and fruit
    c. Meat and fish
    d. Excessive sweets

15. Select the recommended servings per day from the meat group.
    a. Zero to one
    b. Two to three
    c. Four to five
    d. Six to seven

16. A substitute for meat can be all of the following EXCEPT:
    a. Bread
    b. Cheese
    c. Eggs
    d. Beans

17. The food guide pyramid recommends the greatest increase in which food group?
    a. Fruit group
    b. Vegetable group
    c. Meat group
    d. Bread, cereal, rice, and pasta group

18. The daily dietary requirement from the milk group for teenagers is:
    a. One serving per day
    b. Three servings per day
    c. Four servings per day
    d. Milk is not required

19. Substitutes for milk are all of the following EXCEPT:
    a. Jell-O
    b. Cheese
    c. Ice cream
    d. Yogurt

20. Vitamin C is found in which food group?
    a. Meat
    b. Fruits and vegetables
    c. Dairy products
    d. Bread and cereal

21. The bread and cereal group supplies the body with which mineral?
    a. Iodine

b. Calcium
c. Iron
d. Potassium

22. Select the recommended daily allowance for the vegetable group.
    a. One to two
    b. Three to five
    c. Six to seven
    d. Eight to nine

23. Which food aids in the prevention of constipation?
    a. Bread
    b. Fruit
    c. Meat
    d. Cheese

24. Select the recommended daily allowance for the bread, rice, pasta, and cereal group.
    a. One to two
    b. Three to five
    c. Six to eleven
    d. Twelve to thirteen

25. A therapeutic diet is best described as all of the following EXCEPT:
    a. Modified
    b. Regular
    c. Special
    d. Restricted

26. Which diet has no food restrictions?
    a. Regular
    b. Low sodium
    c. Diabetic
    d. Soft

27. Select the food restriction for a diabetic diet.
    a. Salt
    b. Sugar
    c. Pepper
    d. Garlic

28. Select the food restriction for a low sodium diet.
    a. Sugar
    b. Garlic
    c. Salt
    d. Pepper

29. Select the food restriction for a bland diet.
    a. Spices
    b. Sugar
    c. Salt
    d. Jell-O

30. Select the appropriate diet for the resident with a chewing disorder.
    a. Regular
    b. Soft
    c. Bland
    d. Pureed

31. Food prepared similar to baby food is a:
    a. Tube feeding diet
    b. Pureed diet
    c. Low-fat diet
    d. Low residue diet

32. Select the appropriate diet for a resident with the diagnosis of hypertension.
    a. Diabetic
    b. Bland
    c. Low sodium
    d. Regular

33. A nasogastric feeding is best described as:
    a. Feeding through a tube leading to the stomach
    b. Feeding slowly with a straw
    c. Feeding soft food through the mouth
    d. Feeding a liquid diet with a large syringe

34. All of the following are performed prior to tray arrival EXCEPT:
    a. Tidy unit
    b. Elevate the head of the bed
    c. Wash the hands and face
    d. Lower the side rail

35. Select the first action of the nurse assistant before placing the food tray at the bedside.
    a. Cut the meat
    b. Close the curtain
    c. Check the armband
    d. Elevate the bed

36. The clock method is used to explain food location to which type of resident?
    a. Blind
    b. Paralyzed
    c. Deaf
    d. Aphasic

37. All of the following are feeding methods EXCEPT:
    a. Offering liquids between food
    b. Rapidly feeding the resident
    c. Using a straw for liquids
    d. Filling the spoon half full

38. To determine the feeding ability of the resident, the nurse assistant should:
    a. Check the tray card
    b. Ask the resident
    c. Observe the resident
    d. Ask the charge nurse

39. Which example is the appropriate method for documenting dietary intake?
    a. Ate all of the food on the plate
    b. Ate more than enough
    c. Ate a sufficient amount
    d. Ate 100 percent of diet

40. All of the following liquids nourish the body cells EXCEPT:
    a. Milk
    b. Water
    c. Juices
    d. Beer

Answers

1. b. The body's process of using food is nutrition.

2. c. A chemical substance in food is a nutrient.

3. a. An individual specializing in residents'

meal preparation is a dietitian.

4. d. Fifty individual nutrients are necessary to build the body.

5. b. Darkness is not necessary for nutrient formation.

6. c. Examples of nutrients are proteins, carbohydrates, vitamins, minerals, and fats. Alcohol is not a nutrient.

7. b. Carbohydrates are necessary for work energy and heat energy for maintenance of body temperature.

8. d. Proteins are nutrients which build and renew body tissue and regulate body functions.

9. a. Fat nutrients carry vitamin A which is necessary to aid in resisting infections of the respiratory tract, mouth, and eyes. Vitamin D is also carried in the fat nutrients, enabling the body to build strong bones and teeth.

10. b. The nutrient that regulates body processes is water.

11. d. Minerals and vitamins build and renew bones, teeth, and other body tissues.

12. c. Vitamins aid in the prevention of night blindness.

13. b. A balanced diet consists of foods from the food guide pyramid. These new guidelines replace the four basic food groups.

14. d. The food guide pyramid consists of bread, cereal, pasta, rice, fruit, vegetables, meat, poultry, and dairy products. Fats, oil, and sweets should be included but used sparingly.

15. b. The necessary daily servings from the meat group are two to three.

16. a. Bread is not a substitute for meat. Eggs, cheese, beans, and nuts can be substituted for meat.

17. d. The food guide pyramid recommends the greatest increase in the bread, cereal, rice, and pasta group. These complex carbohydrate foods are an important source of energy and are low in calories.

18. c. The recommended daily allowance from the milk group for a teenager is three servings.

19. a. Jello is not a substitute for milk. Any dairy product can be a substitute.

20. b. Vitamin C is found in the fruit and vegetable food group.

21. c. The bread and cereal group supplies the body with the mineral iron.

22. b. The recommended daily allowance for the vegetable group is three to five servings.

23. b. Fruits and vegetables aid in prevention of constipation.

24. c. The recommended daily allowance for the bread, cereal, rice, and pasta group is six to eleven servings.

25. b. A therapeutic diet can be a modified, special, or restricted diet.

26. a. A regular diet has no food restrictions.

27. b. The food restriction for a diabetic diet is sugar.

28. c. The food restriction for a low sodium diet is salt.

29. a. The food restriction for a bland diet is spices. No highly seasoned foods are allowed.

30. d. A pureed diet is ordered for the resident with a chewing difficulty.

31. b. Food blended to a semiliquid form, similar to baby food, is pureed.

32. c. A resident with the diagnosis of hypertension is given a low sodium diet or no salt.

33. a. A nasogastric feeding is best described as a tube inserted through the nose into the stomach. Liquid feedings are given through the tube, providing adequate nutrition.

34. d. The side rail should be in place to prevent falling. The resident's hands and face should be washed. The bedpan or bathroom is offered and the bed elevated if tolerated.

35. c. Before giving the resident the tray, you must check the armband to insure the right resident.

36. a. The clock method is identifying food on the tray according to the clock. For example; 12-eggs, 3-bacon, 6-toast, and 9-juice.

37. b. The resident is fed slowly. Never rapidly feed the resident, as it may cause choking.

38. c. To determine the feeding ability, observe the resident; if difficulty is observed, assist the resident and report the information to the charge nurse.

39. d. To document food intake, use percentage amounts. For example: 100 percent, 75 percent, 50 percent, 25 percent or 0.

40. d. Milk, water, juices, etc., have nutritious value. Alcohol has no valuable nutrient necessary to the body.

9

Body Systems and Conditions

DIRECTIONS: Each question contains suggested responses. Select the one best response to each question.

ANSWERS: See answers at the end of the questions.

1. Anatomy refers to which of the following?
   a. Body conditions
   b. Body movement
   c. Body structures
   d. Body functions

2. Physiology refers to which of the following?
   a. Body functions
   b. Body conditions
   c. Body movement
   d. Body structures

3. The fundamental building blocks of the body are best described as:
   a. Tissues
   b. Cells
   c. Organs
   d. Systems

4. All of the following are parts of the cell EXCEPT:
   a. Cell membrane
   b. Nucleus
   c. Cavities
   d. Cytoplasm

5. A group of cells form which of the following?
   a. Organs
   b. Systems
   c. Human body
   d. Tissues

6. Organs are best described as:
   a. Groups of cells
   b. Groups of tissues
   c. Groups of systems
   d. Groups of vessels

7. Select the appropriate number of systems in the human body.
   a. Eight
   b. Nine
   c. Ten
   d. Eleven

8. Which one of the following systems directs the body's activity?
   a. Nervous
   b. Circulatory
   c. Muscular
   d. Excretory

9. Which one of the following systems gives support to the body?
   a. Integumentary
   b. Skeletal
   c. Muscular
   d. Gastrointestinal

10. Which one of the following systems breaks down food?
    a. Circulatory
    b. Endocrine
    c. Respiratory
    d. Gastrointestinal

11. Which one of the following systems transports oxygen and nutrients and gets rid of waste?
    a. Excretory
    b. Circulatory
    c. Endocrine
    d. Nervous

12. Which system is responsible for the first line of defense against infections?
    a. Integumentary
    b. Skeletal
    c. Gastrointestinal
    d. Nervous

13. Which system is responsible for the reproduction of human life?
    a. Muscular
    b. Circulatory
    c. Reproductive
    d. Respiratory

14. The endocrine system is best described as a:
    a. Hormone system
    b. Motion system
    c. Infection control system
    d. Temperature control system

15. The trachea is located in which system?
    a. Nervous
    b. Excretory
    c. Respiratory
    d. Circulatory

16. The muscular system is responsible for which one of the following?
    a. Support and body protection
    b. Body movement
    c. Elimination
    d. Body metabolism

17. Which two systems are activated during cardiopulmonary resuscitation?
    a. Circulatory and respiratory
    b. Excretory and endocrine
    c. Nervous and integumentary
    d. Circulatory and reproductive

18. The primary purpose of the endocrine system is which one of the following?
    a. Protection from infection
    b. Regulation of body temperature
    c. Elimination of waste products
    d. Hormone secretion

19. Which system's primary functions are support and protection?
    a. Muscular
    b. Skeletal
    c. Nervous
    d. Gastrointestinal

20. Select the appropriate system which allows body movement.
    a. Circulatory
    b. Endocrine
    c. Muscular
    d. Reproductive

21. Select the system which removes waste in the form of urine.
    a. Excretory
    b. Digestive
    c. Respiratory
    d. Integumentary

22. Which one of the following organs in the female reproductive system produces estrogen and progesterone?
    a. Uterus
    b. Ovaries
    c. Fallopian tubes
    d. Labia

23. Select the system which produces hair and nails.
    a. Nervous
    b. Circulatory
    c. Skeletal
    d. Integumentary

24. Select the appropriate system which directs body activity.
    a. Circulatory
    b. Skeletal
    c. Nervous
    d. Muscular

25. A cerebral vascular accident (CVA) is best described as a:
    a. Stroke
    b. Rash
    c. Abrasion
    d. Back injury

26. All of the following can be side effects of a stroke EXCEPT:
    a. Paralysis
    b. Aphasia
    c. Diabetes
    d. Confusion

27. Select the appropriate condition which decreases production of insulin.
    a. Hypertension
    b. Diabetes
    c. Stroke
    d. Cardiac arrest

28. Hypertension is best described as:
    a. High blood sugar
    b. Low blood sugar
    c. Low blood pressure
    d. High blood pressure

29. All of the following are treatments for hypertension EXCEPT:
   a. Medication
   b. Salt intake
   c. Monitoring blood pressure
   d. Low sodium diet

30. A confused, wandering resident is typical of:
   a. Hypertension
   b. Choking victim
   c. Alzheimer's disease
   d. Diabetes

31. Malignancy is best described as:
   a. Cancer
   b. Noncancerous
   c. Trauma
   d. Birth defect

32. Select the appropriate term for a broken bone.
   a. Contracture
   b. Fracture
   c. Dislocation
   d. Sprain

33. Arthritis is best described as a:
   a. Joint sprain
   b. Bone fracture
   c. Disease of the joint
   d. Muscle strain

34. Acquired immune deficiency syndrome (AIDS) is best described as the:
   a. Body's inability to fight infections
   b. Body's inability to digest food
   c. Body's inability to eliminate waste
   d. Body's inability to circulate blood

35. Pneumonia is best described as a:
   a. Infection in the reproductive system
   b. Infection in the excretory system
   c. Infection in the digestive system
   d. Infection in the respiratory system

36. Edema is best described as a:
   a. Rash
   b. Abrasion
   c. Swelling
   d. Treatment

37. Cyanosis is best described as a:
   a. Yellowish discoloration of the skin
   b. Bluish discoloration of the skin
   c. Reddish discoloration of the skin
   d. Normal skin tone

38. Jaundice is best described as:
   a. Moisture on the skin
   b. Reddish skin tone
   c. Yellowish skin tone
   d. Bluish skin tone

39. Convulsions are best described as all of the following EXCEPT:
   a. Seizures
   b. Spasms of the body
   c. Jerking movements of the body
   d. Contagious

40. Select the appropriate statement to describe a contracture.
   a. Locked or stiff joint
   b. Dislocated joint
   c. Sprained joint
   d. Moveable joint

Answers

1. c. Anatomy is the study of body structures.

2. a. Physiology is the study of the body functions.

3. b. Cells are the fundamental building blocks of the human body.

4. c. The cell membrane, nucleus, and cytoplasm are parts of the cell.

5. d. Tissues are formed from groups of cells.

6. b. Body organs are formed from groups of tissues.

7. c. The human body has 10 systems which are separate but work together.

8. a. The nervous system controls the body's activity. The brain directs all activity by way of the spinal cord and nerves.

9. b. The skeletal system gives shape and supports the organ within the human body.

10. d. The gastrointestinal or digestive system is responsible for the breakdown and utilization of food.

11. b. The circulatory system is responsible for transporting oxygen and nutrients and for removal of waste products from the body.

12. a. The integumentary system (skin) is the first line of defense against infections. The other functions are body temperature control, lubrication, body hair, and nail formation.

13. c. The reproductive system is responsible for reproduction of a human life. Sperm from the male and an ovum or egg from the female are united.

14. a. The endocrine system produces hormones necessary for bodily processes.

15. c. The trachea is the windpipe and is found in the respiratory system.

16. b. The muscular system makes body movement possible.

17. a. During cardiopulmonary resuscitation (CPR) the two systems used are the circulatory and respiratory systems.

18. d. The primary function of the endocrine System is hormone production.

19. b. The primary functions of the skeletal system are support and protection.

20. c. The primary function of the muscular system is body movement.

21. a. The excretory (urinary) system's primary function is the removal of waste in the form of urine.

22. b. The ovaries in the female reproductive system produce estrogen and progesterone to maintain normal female functions.

23. d. The integumentary system is responsible for the formation of hair and nails.

24. c. The nervous system directs body activity.

25. a. A cerebral vascular accident (CVA) is a stroke.

26. c. Paralysis, aphasia, and confusion are side effects. Diabetes is a disease, not a side effect of a CVA.

27. b. Diabetes is a condition affecting the pancreas that causes a decrease or absence of insulin, which is necessary to regulate blood sugar levels.

28. d. Hypertension is the same as high blood pressure.

29. b. Daily medication, frequent blood pressure monitoring, and a low sodium diet are treatments. The intake of salt is discouraged.

30. c. The characteristics of an Alzheimer's resident are confusion and wandering.

31. a. Malignancy is another name for cancer. Benign means noncancerous.

32. b. A broken bone is a fracture.

33. c. Arthritis is a disease of the joint.

34. a. Acquired immune deficiency syndrome (AIDS) is the body's inability to fight infections.

35. d. Pneumonia is an inflammation in the respiratory system.

36. c. Edema is swelling, commonly seen in the extremities.

37. b. Cyanosis is a bluish discoloration of the skin, commonly seen in the lips, hands, and feet.

38. c. Jaundice is a yellowish skin tone also seen in the eyes.

39. d. Convulsions are seizures, spasms of the body and can be jerking movements. Convulsions are not contagious.

40. a. A contracture is a stiff or locked joint.

10

Vital Signs: Treatment and Procedure

DIRECTIONS: Each question contains four suggested responses. Select the one best response to each question.

ANSWERS: See answers at the end of the questions.

1. Vital signs are best described as
   a. Temperature, pulse, and respiration
   b. Blood pressure, respiration, temperature, and pulse
   c. Blood pressure, temperature, and pulse
   d. Blood pressure, respiration, and temperature

2. Which one of the following vital signs measures the amount of force necessary to circulate the blood?
   a. Temperature
   b. Pulse
   c. Blood pressure
   d. Respiration

3. Select the artery used to measure the blood pressure.
   a. Radial
   b. Pulmonary
   c. Carotid
   d. Brachial

4. Select the listening device used to monitor the blood pressure.
   a. Sphygmomanometer
   b. Stethoscope
   c. Cuff
   d. Thermometer

5. Select the piece of equipment used in blood pressure monitoring that requires cleansing before use.
   a. Bulb
   b. Tubing
   c. Cuff
   d. Ear piece

6. Select the blood pressure reading indicating hypotension.
   a. 90/50
   b. 90/60
   c. 100/60
   d. 110/60

7. Select the blood pressure reading indicating hypertension.
   a. 120/86
   b. 130/80
   c. 140/90
   d. 160/92

8. All of the following describe the diastolic reading EXCEPT:
   a. Its normal range is 60 to 90.
   b. It is the bottom number.
   c. It is the top number.
   d. It can be elevated.

9. Select the systolic reading which indicates hypertension.
   a. 152/90
   b. 120/80
   c. 140/90
   d. 130/70

10. Prolonged hypertension can lead to which condition?
    a. Heart attack
    b. Stroke
    c. Diabetes
    d. Seizure

11. Select the appropriate vital sign which measures the amount of heat in the body.
    a. Blood pressure
    b. Respiration
    c. Pulse
    d. Temperature

12. Select the piece of equipment necessary to measure the amount of heat in the body.
    a. Thermometer
    b. Stethoscope
    c. Sphygmomanometer
    d. Watch with a second hand

13. All of the following are ways to obtain the temperature EXCEPT:
    a. Axillary
    b. Oral
    c. Rectal
    d. Hand (by touch)

14. Select the most convenient temperature method.
    a. Oral
    b. Rectal
    c. Axillary
    d. Femoral

15. Select the least convenient temperature method.
    a. Axillary
    b. Rectal
    c. Oral
    d. Femoral

16. Which one of the following should the nurse assistant do first before placing a thermometer in the mouth?
    a. Inspect the thermometer for cracks.
    b. Hold the thermometer straight.
    c. Shake the thermometer below 95°F.
    d. Check the resident skin temperature.

17. Select the normal range for an oral temperature reading.
    a. 97.6°F to 99°F
    b. 98.6°F to 100°F
    c. 96°F to 98°F
    d. 95°F to 99°F

18. What should the nurse assistant understand regarding eating and oral temperature taking?
    a. Wait at least 1 hour.
    b. Wait at least 15 minutes.
    c. Wait at least 45 minutes.
    d. There is no need to wait.

19. Select the appropriate action of the nurse assistant before taking an axillary temperature.
    a. Shave the armpit.
    b. Lubricate the thermometer.
    c. Wash the thermometer with hot water.
    d. Dry the armpit.

20. All of the following types of residents would have their temperature taken orally EXCEPT:
    a. Residents with recent rectal surgery
    b. Residents receiving oxygen

    c. Teenage resident
    d. Residents with diarrhea

21. Select the appropriate time frame for a rectal temperature.
    a. 3 to 4 minutes
    b. 5 to 7 minutes
    c. 6 to 8 minutes
    d. 9 to 10 minutes

22. Regarding rectal temperatures the nurse assistant should do all the following actions EXCEPT:
    a. Insert the thermometer 1 inch and hold
    b. Wear gloves
    c. Leave the resident unattended
    d. Lubricate the thermometer tip

23. Select the vital sign which indicates how fast the blood is circulating in the body.
    a. Blood pressure
    b. Temperature
    c. Respiration
    d. Pulse

24. Select the artery used to monitor the pulse rate.
    a. Brachial
    b. Radial
    c. Carotid
    d. Femoral

25. Select the appropriate normal pulse range.
    a. 72 to 80
    b. 85 to 90
    c. 90 to 100
    d. 60 to 70

26. Select the appropriate piece of equipment necessary to obtain the pulse rate.
    a. Watch with no second hand
    b. Stethoscope
    c. Watch with a second hand
    d. Sphygmomanometer

27. An apical pulse is monitored at which location?
    a. Wrist area
    b. Neck area
    c. Right lower heart area
    d. Left lower heart area

28. Which vital sign is taken without the resident being aware?
    a. Pulse
    b. Respiration
    c. Temperature
    d. Blood pressure

29. Select the normal range for the respiratory rate.
    a. 16 to 20
    b. 12 to 15
    c. 19 to 24
    d. 17 to 22

30. Which one of the following would be an abnormal respiratory rate?
    a. 24
    b. 18
    c. 20
    d. 16

31. Respiration is best described as:
    a. One inhale
    b. One exhale
    c. One inhale and one exhale
    d. Two inhales and two exhales

32. A treatment to relieve constipation is best described as:
    a. Sitz bath
    b. Bladder irrigation
    c. Enema
    d. Edema

33. All of the following treatments can reduce swelling EXCEPT:
    a. Cold compress
    b. Elevation
    c. Cold soaks
    d. Hot compress

34. Select the appropriate treatment to relieve abdominal flatus (gas).
    a. Harris flush
    b. Sitz bath
    c. Coughing and deep breathing
    d. Repositioning every 2 hours

35. A treatment to promote healing to the perineal area is best described as:
    a. Enema
    b. Sitz bath
    c. Vaginal douche
    d. Harris flush

36. Select the appropriate procedure which monitors sugar and acetone in the urine.
    a. Routine urinalysis
    b. Midstream
    c. Clinitest
    d. Intake and Output

37. Select the appropriate time to collect a sputum specimen.
    a. Late morning
    b. Early morning
    c. Afternoon
    d. Bedtime

38. Isolation procedure is all of the following EXCEPT:
    a. Gloves
    b. Disposable eating utensils
    c. Doublebagging
    d. Room door left open

39. All of the following are postoperative procedures EXCEPT:
    a. Close observation of surgical site
    b. Turning, deep breathing, and coughing
    c. Lack of movement to allow the resident to rest
    d. Elastic stockings

40. Select the appropriate observation method when caring for a resident receiving intravenous therapy.
    a. Observe the flow, and report any problems
    b. Observe the amount of time it takes for the solution to flow in
    c. Observe only the needle sites
    d. No observation necessary, the charge nurse will monitor the intravenous therapy

Answers

1. b. The vital signs are blood pressure, temperature, pulse, and respiration. These are necessary for life, and tell the doctor how the body is functioning.

2. c. The blood pressure measures the amount of force necessary to circulate the blood through the body.

3. d. The brachial artery is used to measure the blood pressure. It is located in the fold of the inner arm.

4. b. The stethoscope is the listening device used in blood pressure monitoring.

5. d. The ear piece should be cleansed with antiseptic solution after use to prevent ear infections.

6. a. Hypotension is low pressure; a blood pressure reading of 90/50 indicates hypotension.

7. d. A blood pressure reading of 160/92 indicates hypertension.

8. c. The diastolic reading of the blood pressure is the bottom number; it can be elevated; and the normal range is 60 to 90.

9. a. The systolic reading indicating hypertension is 152/90. The top number is out of the normal range. The normal range for systolic pressure is 90 to 140.

10. b. Prolonged hypertension can lead to a stroke.

11. d. The vital sign which measures the amount of heat in the body is the temperature.

12. a. The equipment necessary is the thermometer. When taking a temperature always use a plastic cover for infection control.

13. d. Touching the resident's skin will not give an accurate temperature reading.

14. a. The most convenient temperature method is oral.

15. b. The least convenient temperature method is the rectal.

16. a. The nurse assistant should inspect the thermometer for cracks.

17. a. The normal range for an oral temperature reading is 97.6ºF to 99ºF.

18. b. The nurse assistant should wait at least 15 minutes after eating, drinking, and smoking. The temperature of foods or drinks can alter the reading.

19. d. The nurse assistant should make sure the armpit is dry.

20. b. A resident receiving oxygen has difficulty breathing. Taking an oral temperature would decrease the resident's ability to breathe through the mouth.

21. a. The time allotted for a rectal temperature is 3 to 4 minutes.

22. c. Never leave the resident unattended with a rectal thermometer in place. The rectal thermometer should be held in place to prevent injury should the resident decide to change positions.

23. d. The pulse gives an indication of how fast the blood is circulating in the body.

24. b. The radial artery at the wrist is used to monitor the pulse rate. The apical pulse is sometimes requested; this is monitored at the lower left portion of the heart.

25. a. The normal range for the pulse is 72 to 80.

26. c. A watch with a second hand is used to monitor the pulse.

27. d. The apical pulse is monitored at the apex of the heart, which is the lower left portion of the heart area.

28. b. The respiration is taken without the resident being aware. If the resident is aware, the breathing pattern could be altered.

29. a. The normal respiratory rate is 16 to 20.

30. a. An abnormal respiratory rate is 24. This rate is out of the normal range of 16 to 20.

31. c. Respiration is best described as one inhale, which is the intake of oxygen (O_2) and one exhale, which is the release of carbon dioxide (CO_2).

32. c. The treatment which relieves constipation is an enema.

33. d. Cold application reduces swelling as the cold constricts the vessels. Hot compresses are not used to reduce swelling because of the dilation of the vessels caused by heat.

34. a. A Harris flush relieves abdominal flatus or gas.

35. b.   The sitz bath dilates the perineal vessels, bringing an increased amount of oxygen and nutrients to the area. This dilation promotes healing of the perineal area.

36. c.   The Clinitest tests the urine for sugar and acetone.

37. b.   A sputum specimen should be obtained in the early morning. This sputum should be a deep coughed mucus specimen.

38. d.   The door is always kept closed during the isolation process.

39. c.   Postoperative procedure is close observation, frequent turning, coughing, and deep breathing. This will help prevent pneumonia caused by a lack of lung inflation. Moving the resident frequently is highly recommended.

40. a.   Monitor the amount and flow of the solution, check the needle site, and watch for tubing kinks.

11

Observation: Reporting and Charting

I. Observations
   a. Types
   b. Purpose

II. Reporting observations
   a. Subjective
   b. Objective
   c. Purpose

III. Documentation or charting
   a. Types
   b. Purpose

IV. Terminology
   a. Key terms
      1. Observation
      2. Subjective observation
      3. Objective observation
      4. Assessment
      5. Confidential
      6. Chart
      7. Charting
      8. Narrative note
      9. Graph
      10. Documentation

DIRECTIONS: Each question contains suggested responses. Select the one best response to each question.

ANSWERS: See answers at the end of the questions.

1. Observation is all of the following *except*:
   a. Appearance of the resident
   b. Actions of the resident
   c. Conversation of the resident
   d. Assumptions of the nurse assistant

2. Select an example of a subjective observation.
   a. "I can't stop coughing."
   b. "I have a headache."
   c. "My leg is swollen."
   d. "My toenails are blue."

3. Select an example of an objective observation.
   a. Red eyes
   b. Chest pain
   c. Abdominal pain
   d. Dizziness

4. An observation of skin inflammation is which one of the following?
   a. Jaundice
   b. Cyanosis
   c. Redness
   d. Colorless

5. Select the appropriate statement for a change in the resident's status.
   a. An old problem
   b. A part of the daily routine
   c. An ongoing problem
   d. A new problem

6. An observation of a bluish discoloration of the skin is best described as:
   a. Inflammation
   b. Cyanosis
   c. Edema
   d. Jaundice

7. Assessment of the resident is best described as all of the following EXCEPT:
   a. Observing the resident from head to toe

   b. Focusing on what the resident reports
   c. Disregarding previous shift report
   d. Vital signs

8. If difficulty in breathing is an observation, the nurse assistant should:
   a. Lower the head of the bed
   b. Elevate the foot of the bed
   c. Discuss the condition with another nurse assistant
   d. Report the condition to the charge nurse immediately

9. Select the appropriate term for a resident who is unable to remember dates, place and time.
   a. Agitated
   b. Alert
   c. Confused
   d. Combative

10. The nurse assistant routinely observes urine for all of the following abnormalities EXCEPT:
    a. Color
    b. pH
    c. Amount
    d. Odor

11. Observations of a soiled bed three times on one shift would indicate which one of the following?
    a. The resident is incontinent
    b. The resident is on intake and output
    c. The resident has an indwelling catheter
    d. The resident is continent

12. Select the first action to be taken if the nurse assistant observes the resident straining while using the bedpan.
    a. Offer the resident a Correctal tablet
    b. Ask the resident, "Are you OK?"
    c. Report straining to the charge nurse
    d. Encourage the resident to eat more vegetables

13. Select the appropriate observation to be made if the resident's feet are swollen.
    a. Emesis

b. Enema

c. Edema

d. Jaundice

14. Which one of the following observations would indicate the resident has insomnia?

a. A restful night

b. Tossing and turning

c. Lethargic

d. Comatose

15. Decubitus ulcers are generally observed on which areas of the body?

a. Bony areas

b. Muscular areas

c. Anterior body

d. Upper body

16. All of the following are observations dealing with breathing EXCEPT:

a. SOB

b. Asthma

c. Dyspnea

d. Combativeness

17. Select the appropriate response if the resident complains of burning while urinating.

a. Take the vital signs and report the problem

b. Increase the amount of fluid intake

c. Decrease the amount of fluid intake

d. Check the odor of the urine

18. Select the appropriate action if the resident complains of extreme weakness and dizziness before a transfer.

a. Complete the transfer and report to the charge nurse

b. Understand that the complaint is normal

c. Discontinue the transfer and report to the charge nurse

d. Ask the visitors to assist with the transfer

19. An observation of dry skin with no skin turgor and excessive thirst could indicate:

a. Aging process

b. Excessive fluid intake

c. Constipation

d. Dehydration

20. Select the appropriate action of the nurse assistant if a painful lump is felt in the resident's abdomen during a bath.

a. Report the lump to another nurse assistant

b. Ask the resident how long the lump has been there

c. Place a cold compress on the lump

d. Notify the doctor.

21. The primary purpose of observation by the nurse assistant is best described as:

a. A method of completing the medical record

b. A method of preventing further decline in the resident's health

c. A method of gathering information for a team conference

d. A method of complying with the nurse's instructions

22. Which one of the following observations would cause the doctor to order antibiotics?

a. Headache

b. Hypertension

c. Burning urination

d. Hypotension

23. All of the following are methods of follow-up after a reported fall EXCEPT:

a. Check skin for bruises or abrasion

b. Monitor the resident's complaints

c. Ask the resident how he or she is feeling

d. Assume the resident is okay

24. Subjective reporting is best described as:

a. What the nurse assistant observes

b. What the resident states

c. What the nurse assistant feels

d. What the roommate said

25. Select the appropriate method for reporting a resident's complaint.

a. Name, problem, bed, and diagnosis

b. Name, room, problem, and medication

c. Name, room, bed, problem, and onset

d. Name, problem, and time started

26. Which one of the following actions is performed before reporting a resident's complaint of abdominal pain?
    a. Take only the temperature
    b. Take the vital signs
    c. Take the blood pressure and temperature
    d. Take only the blood pressure

27. Objective reporting is best described as:
    a. What the nurse assistant observes
    b. What the resident feels
    c. What the resident says
    d. What the nurse assistant thinks

28. Which one of the following resident's actions should be reported immediately?
    a. Laughing
    b. Incontinence
    c. Combative behavior
    d. Continuous hand clapping.

29. Resident's complaints are reported to which one of the following?
    a. Supervisor
    b. Charge nurse
    c. Ward clerk
    d. Director of nurses

30. All of the following are purposes for reporting a resident's complaints EXCEPT:
    a. To keep the charge nurse busy
    b. To protect the resident
    c. To get the complaint resolved
    d. To prevent further decline in the resident's health

31. A written record containing information about the resident's care is best described as:
    a. A diary
    b. An autobiography
    c. A legal document
    d. A nonlegal document

32. Confidentiality is best described as:
    a. Keeping a resident's medical record private
    b. Allowing friends to review the chart
    c. Discussing the resident's medical history with visitors
    d. Open media discussions about the resident's care

33. All of the following are principles for charting EXCEPT:
    a. Entries must be in ink
    b. Leave blank spaces
    c. Entries must be signed with first initial, last name, and title
    d. Entries must be in chronological order

34. Charting is best described as:
    a. Accurate written information about the care given and tolerance
    b. Nonfactual written information about the resident's care
    c. Written information regarding only how the resident responds to care
    d. Unreadable entries about the resident care

35. Narrative charting is best described as:
    a. Writing one problem per shift
    b. Short form charting
    c. Essay style
    d. Entries every 4 hours

36. A graph sheet is best described as:
    a. A dotted record of vital signs
    b. A treatment record
    c. An intake and output record
    d. A written nurse's note of care given

37. Select the appropriate format for short form charting.
    a. Answering yes or no to all care provided and signing
    b. Narrative nurse assistant's note after all care
    c. A detailed summary of care given
    d. A short estimation of care given

38. Select the appropriate statement regarding correction of a charting error
    a. Erase the error and rewrite
    b. Blacken the entire error and rewrite
    c. Use whiteout, initial, and rewrite
    d. Draw one line through the error, initial, and rewrite.

39. All of the following are purposes of the chart EXCEPT:

   a. To give directions for care according to the physician's orders

   b. To verify if orders have been followed

   c. To have an ongoing record of most of the care given

   d. To show resident tolerance and progress

while hospitalized

40. All of the following are purposes for the nurse assistant's documentation EXCEPT:

   a. To document observations of the resident's appearance and complaints

   b. To document reactions to care provided

   c. To document all care provided

   d. To document estimation of care provided

Answers

1. d. Observations are what you actually see, hear, and touch.

2. b. An example of a subjective observation is, "I have a headache." Subjective observations are what the resident feels and states.

3. a. An objective observation is what you can see, such as red eyes.

4. c. An observation of a skin inflammation is redness.

5. d. A change in the resident's status is a new problem. An example might be cystitis.

6. b. An observation of a bluish discoloration of the skin is cyanosis.

7. c. Assessment is observation from the resident's head to toe. The resident's complaints, vital signs, and the previous shift's report can assist the nurse assistant in assessing the resident.

8. d. Difficulty breathing is an observation that the nurse assistant should report to the charge nurse immediately.

9. c. If the resident is unaware of the date, place, and time, the resident is said to be confused and disoriented.

10. b. The pH is done in the lab. Observation of the urine includes color, amount, odor, and any other abnormalities.

11. a. A soiled bed at least three times on your shift would suggest the resident is incontinent. Incontinence is lack of control of bowel or bladder.

12. b. The first action of the nurse assistant is to ask the resident if he or she is all right.

13. c. Edema is swelling commonly seen in feet, legs, and hands.

14. b. Frequent tossing and turning through the night, an inability to fall asleep, and restlessness indicate insomnia.

15. a. Decubitus ulcers are commonly seen on the bony areas of the body. For examples, coccyx, hips, elbows, shoulder blades, ankles, and heels.

16. d. Combativeness is uncooperative behavior. Shortness of breath (SOB), asthma, and dyspnea are breathing observations.

17. a. Take the vital signs and report the problem.

18. c. Discontinue the transfer and notify the charge nurse for further instructions.

19. d. Dehydration is an observation associated with dry skin, no skin turgor, and excessive thirst.

20. b. If a painful lump is felt, ask the resident how long the problem has existed and then report the information to the charge nurse.

21. b. The primary purpose of observation is as a method of preventing further decline in the resident's health.

22. c. An observation of the resident's complaint of burning when urinating could indicate an infection in the urinary tract. The physician would order a urinalysis to be followed by antibiotics.

23. d. Follow-up after a fall is close observation, a skin check for bruises and abrasions, and a check of vital signs.

24. b. Subjective observations and reporting are what the resident states. An example is, "I have a headache."

25. c. Information necessary when reporting resident's complaints is name, room, bed, problem, and onset.

26. b. The nurse assistant should take the vital signs and report the complaint of abdominal pain to the charge nurse.

27. a. Objective reporting is what the nurse assistant observes.

28. c. Combative behavior must be reported. The resident could injure himself or herself or others.

29. b. The nurse assistant should report resident's complaints to the charge nurse.

30. a. Keeping the charge nurse busy is not the purpose of reporting complaints. To prevent further decline in the health of the resident is the primary purpose.

31. c. The resident's record containing information and care given is a legal document and can be used in court.

32. a. Confidentiality is keeping the resident's medical record private.

33. b. Blank spaces are never left in the nurse's note.

34. a. Charting is accurate written information about the care given and the resident's response.

35. c. Narrative charting is essay style and can be documented at any interval.

36. a. A graph sheet is a dotted record of vital signs. The graph shows the increase or decrease of the vital signs.

37. a. Short form charting is answering yes or no; sometimes checks are used to indicate care given.

38. d. To correct charting errors, the nurse assistant should draw one line through the error, initial, and rewrite.

39. c. The primary purpose of the chart or medical records is to give direction for care, to verify orders, and to reflect resident's tolerance to progress with the care given.

40. d. The purpose for charting or documenting is to have an ongoing record of all of the care given to the resident, with his or her tolerance and progress.

12

Admissions, Discharges, and Rehabilitation

I. Admission procedure
   a. Types
   b. Purpose

II. Discharges
   a. Definition
   b. Procedure

III. Rehabilitation
   a. Key terms
      1. Rehabilitation
      2. Rehabilitation team
      3. Physical therapist
      4. Occupational therapist
      5. Speech therapist
      6. Dressing technique
      7. Activities of daily living (ADL)
      8. Independence
      9. Range of motion (ROM)
     10. Bowel and bladder training

DIRECTIONS: Each question contains four suggested responses. Select the one best response to each question.

ANSWERS: See answers at the end of the questions.

1. Admission is best described as:
   a. Policy and procedures for discharge
   b. Entry process into the health care setting
   c. Referring residents to an outside specialist
   d. Introduction to home health care for the homebound resident

2. Select the appropriate action of the nurse assistant to begin the admission process.
   a. Check the room
   b. Speak to the physician
   c. Change the linen on the bed
   d. Post a new admission sign on the door

3. A new resident is waiting in the room to be admitted. Select the appropriate action of the nurse assistant.
   a. Go to lunch; admit the resident later
   b. Assign the admission to your coworker
   c. Allow the resident to wait 30 minutes
   d. Go to the room; greet and admit the resident

4. Comfort measures for the newly admitted resident are all of the following EXCEPT:
   a. Orientation to hospital policies
   b. Introduction to the roommate
   c. Disinterested nurse assistant
   d. Explanation of the signal light

5. A newly admitted resident requests food. Select the appropriate response by the nurse assistant.
   a. Go to the kitchen; request a regular diet
   b. Report the information to the charge nurse
   c. Give the resident a cup of soup
   d. Explain to the resident he or she is NPO

6. Select the appropriate method to keep a record of the resident's valuables.
   a. Report verbally to the charge nurse
   b. List the valuables on the nurse's note

   c. Record on your pocket note pad
   d. Tell your coworker to list the valuables

7. Standard responsibilities of the nurse assistant during admission are all of the following EXCEPT:
   a. Vital signs
   b. Height and weight
   c. Body check
   d. Diagnosis explanation

8. An open red area is observed on the coccyx during the admission body check. Select the appropriate term.
   a. Stage 1 decubitus
   b. Stage 2 decubitus
   c. Stage 3 decubitus
   d. Stage 4 decubitus

9. An admission checklist is completed by which staff member?
   a. Doctor
   b. Charge nurse
   c. LVN
   d. Nurse assistant

10. A resident begins to cry during the admission process. Select the appropriate response.
    a. Tell the resident to stop crying
    b. Ignore the crying and continue the admission process
    c. Encourage the resident to express feelings
    d. Ask the family member why the resident is crying

11. Which of the following names should be used when communicating with the resident?
    a. Resident's first name
    b. Resident's last name
    c. Papa or mama
    d. Sweetie or honey

12. Which items are placed at the newly admitted resident's bedside?
    a. Water pitcher, wash basin, and urinal or bedpan

b. Water pitcher, cup, wash basin, and bedpan

c. Pitcher of water, cup, wash basin, and bedpan

d. Empty water pitcher, cup, bedpan or urinal, wash basin, and emesis basin

13. Dress code for the newly admitted resident is which one of the following?
    a. Gown or pajamas
    b. Slacks, shirt, or blouse
    c. Jogging suit
    d. Housecoat and slippers

14. Select the appropriate method to measure the height of a resident on complete bed rest.
    a. Place the resident on the side; use the tape measure to get the height.
    b. Place the resident on the upright scale.
    c. Ask the resident the correct height.
    d. Place the resident on the back; mark head and feet; and roll to the side and measure with tape measure.

15. All of the following are proper descriptions of the resident's jewelry EXCEPT:
    a. Yellow metal with white stone
    b. Grey metal with two large red stones
    c. Gold ring with a large diamond
    d. Yellow chain with a small yellow pendant

16. Anxiety and agitation are observed during the admission process. Describe the action of the resident.
    a. Calm
    b. Cooperative
    c. Sleepy and unresponsive
    d. Nervous and uncooperative

17. Select the appropriate method to handle medications brought from home by the resident.
    a. Send the medication home with the family.
    b. Allow the resident to keep the medication.
    c. Give the medication to the charge nurse.
    d. List all medication and dispose with a witness present.

18. An artificial limb is best described as:
    a. A hearing aid
    b. Partial or full dentures
    c. A lower extremity
    d. A cane

19. Select the appropriate method to verify the resident's allergies
    a. Ask the doctor
    b. Ask the resident
    c. Ask a friend
    d. Ask the roommate

20. Select the appropriate action of the nurse assistant after completing the admission process.
    a. Report findings to the physician
    b. Discuss findings with the ward clerk
    c. Only document information
    d. Report findings to the charge nurse

21. Initial discharge planning begins at which stage?
    a. Beginning of hospitalization
    b. Middle of hospitalization
    c. Ending of hospitalization
    d. Once the resident decides to leave the hospital

22. Discharge is best described as:
    a. Procedure for admission into a health care setting
    b. Procedure for leaving a health care setting
    c. Procedure for entry into another unit
    d. A diagnostic procedure

23. A discharge order is written by which one of the following?
    a. Ward clerk
    b. Charge nurse
    c. Physician
    d. Director of nurses

24. Select the appropriate abbreviation to refer to a resident leaving the health care setting without permission.
    a. ADA
    b. AMA
    c. AGA
    d. ANA

25. Select the appropriate action prior to discharging the resident.
    a. Explain the discharge procedure.

b. Gather all the resident's belongings and place them into a bag

c. Check the discharge order

d. Check the arm band

26. All of the following are the responsibility of the nurse assistant prior to discharge EXCEPT:
    a. Checking the arm band
    b. Completing the discharge checklist
    c. Giving the resident the release form
    d. Assisting the resident to the discharge area in a wheelchair

27. All of the following are appropriate methods to assist residents to the discharge pickup area EXCEPT:
    a. Allowing the resident to ambulate
    b. Using a wheelchair
    c. Using a stretcher
    d. Using a gurney

28. Rehabilitation is best described as all of the following EXCEPT:
    a. Assisting the resident to recover to as normal state as possible
    b. Assisting the resident physically, emotionally, socially, and spiritually during the recovery period
    c. Allowing the resident to do as much as possible
    d. Encouraging the resident to be dependent

29. All of the following are functions of the rehabilitation team EXCEPT:
    a. Develop an individual rehabilitation plan
    b. Motivation of the mind and body
    c. Promotion of inactivity
    d. Encourage daily participation

30. A primary function of the physical therapist is:
    a. To assist the resident with activities of motion
    b. To assist the resident with the thought process
    c. To assist the resident with nutrition
    d. To assist the resident with performing activities of daily living

31. Which member of the rehabilitation team assists with activities of daily living?
    a. Speech therapist
    b. Occupational therapist
    c. Physical therapist
    d. Psychologist

32. Select the appropriate method for dressing a resident with a weak right or left side.
    a. Dress the affected side first.
    b. Dress the unaffected side first.
    c. Allow the resident to decide.
    d. Either side may be first; it does not matter.

33. Select the appropriate therapist to assist the resident with a condition of aphasia.
    a. Occupational therapist
    b. Speech therapist
    c. Psychologist
    d. Physical therapist

34. Select the appropriate response if the resident becomes frustrated while trying to communicate verbally.
    a. Offer a pad and pencil
    b. Ignore the resident's frustration
    c. Assume what the resident is saying
    d. Explain to the resident that it's not your fault

35. All of the following consist of activities of daily living skills (ADL) EXCEPT:
    a. Shopping
    b. Nutrition
    c. Grooming
    d. Toileting

36. Select the appropriate action to encourage the resident to be as independent as possible.
    a. Do everything for the resident to save time
    b. Allow the residents to perform their own tasks
    c. Constantly remind the residents of their disabilities
    d. Show little patience

37. A resident with (R) right-sided weakness has difficulty holding a spoon. Select the appropriate action of the nurse assistant.
    a. Feed the resident

b. Give the resident a spoon with an easy-grip handle

c. Encourage the resident to try harder

d. Tape the spoon to the resident's hand

38. Range of motion prevents which one of the following conditions?
    a. Rashes
    b. Bruises
    c. Contractures
    d. Abrasions

39. Select the appropriate method to perform range of motion.
    a. Exercise each joint four times
    b. Exercise each joint three times
    c. Exercise each joint two times
    d. Exercise each joint one time

40. Select the appropriate method for a resident's bowel and bladder retraining.
    a. Administer daily laxatives
    b. Offer the bedpan every 3 hours
    c. Assist to the bathroom or offer the bedpan every 4 hours
    d. Offer the bedpan or assist to the bathroom every 2 hours

Answers

1. b. Admission is the entry process before hospitalization.

2. a. The nurse assistant should always check the room and make sure the room is ready to receive the new resident.

3. d. The nurse assistant should go promptly to the room and greet the resident. Introduce yourself and if a roommate is present, introduce the roommate. This will aid in making the resident feel comfortable.

4. c. The nurse assistant should never appear disinterested because this can cause the resident additional feelings of discomfort.

5. b. Report to the charge nurse and allow the charge nurse to make the decision after reviewing the physician's admission orders.

6. b. To keep a record of the resident's valuables, list them on the admission nurse's note.

7. d. Standard admission responsibilities of the nurse assistant are vital signs, body check for bruises, abrasions, and decubitus. The height and weight are also obtained.

8. b. An open red area is a stage 2 decubitus.

9. d. The admission checklist is completed by the nurse assistant.

10. c. Encourage the resident to express feelings.

11. b. Address the resident with Mr. or Ms. and his or her last name, this is respectful. Never call the resident honey, sweetie, papa, or mama.

12. d. An empty water pitcher should be placed at the resident's bedside until the charge nurse can verify that the resident can have water. Bedside utensils consist of cup, bedpan, or urinal, wash basin and emesis basin.

13. a. Dress code is a gown to allow easy observations during the body check and pajamas after the procedure.

14. d. To check the height of a resident on complete bed rest, place the resident on his or her back; mark the head and feet with a line on the sheet, and then roll the resident to his or her side and measure the marks with a tape measure.

15. c. Never use terms such as gold or diamonds. Always use terms such as yellow metal, grey metal, red stone, white stone, or green stone.

16. d. Anxiety and agitation are characteristic of the nervous, uncooperative resident.

17. c. All medication brought in with the resident should be given to the charge nurse.

18. c. An artificial limb is another name for an upper or lower extremity.

19. b. If the resident is alert, you may ask the resident to verify allergies.

20. d. After the admission process the nurse assistant should report findings to the charge nurse.

21. a. Initial discharge planning begins on admission.

22. b. Discharge is the procedure for leaving the health care setting.

23. c. A discharge order is written by the physician.

24. b. The abbreviation for a resident leaving the health care setting without permission is called AMA (against medical advice).

25. c. Verify the discharge order before you start the discharge process.

26. c. The release form is never given to the resident. This form is given to the charge nurse to be placed in the resident's chart.

27. a. The resident is assisted to the discharge area in a wheelchair. The resident is never allowed to ambulate to the area.

28. d. Rehabilitation is encouraging the resident to be independent, to do as much for themselves as possible.

29. c. Promotion of inactivity is not a function of the rehabilitation team. The rehabilitation team promotes activity, develops individual plans for recovery, and deals with the holistic approach. The entire body is involved in the rehabilitation process.

30. a. The physical therapist assists the resident with activities of motion.

31. b. The occupational therapist assists the resident with activities of daily living (ADL) skills.

32. a. The affected side is dressed first.

33. b. A speech therapist deals with speech problems, such as aphasia, slurred speech, or any speaking difficulty.

34. a. A pad and pencil will allow the resident to write down information requested.

35. a. Activities of daily living (ADL) skills are grooming, nutrition, bathing, and toileting.

36. b. To encourage a resident's independence allow the resident to perform as much of his or her own care as possible.

37. b. Give the resident an easy-grip handled spoon. This will allow the resident to hold the spoon for longer intervals.

38. c. Range of motion prevents contracture, which is the locking or stiffening of a joint from lack of movement.

39. b. Each joint should be exercised at least three times.

40. d. The resident should be offered the bedpan or assisted to the bathroom every 2 hours during bowel and bladder retraining.

13

Dying, Death, and Postmortem Care

DIRECTIONS: Each question contains four suggested responses. Select the one best response to each question.

ANSWERS: See answers at the end of the questions.

1. A terminal condition is best described as:
   a. A disease or condition that is likely to cause death
   b. A condition which is treated with surgery
   c. A condition which is treated with medication
   d. A disease or condition from which the resident will fully recover with time

2. Select the appropriate response if the terminal resident states, "Am I going to die?"
   a. Tell the resident very soon.
   b. Tell the resident do not worry about it.
   c. Tell the resident we all have to die.
   d. Ask the resident if he or she would like to speak with the charge nurse.

3. Hospice is best described as:
   a. In-home professional medical care for terminal residents
   b. Out-patient care through the clinic
   c. Special care in the health care setting
   d. A name for a dying resident

4. Select the primary purpose of hospice care.
   a. Emotional support and comfort to resident and family
   b. Long-term nursing care
   c. Assisting as little as possible
   d. Encouraging family members to handle their problems alone

5. Hospice services are available to residents and family at which intervals?
   a. 8:00 A.M. to 4:00 P.M.
   b. 7:00 A.M. to 7:00 P.M.
   c. Only day hours
   d. Whenever necessary

6. A dying resident is talking to you about dying. Select the appropriate response.
   a. Reassure the resident he or she is not dying
   b. Listen and allow the resident to express his or her feeling
   c. Tell the resident he or she will get better
   d. Immediately tell the resident that you cannot discuss the matter

7. Select the appropriate action of the nurse assistant if the terminal resident continues to turn on the call signal.
   a. Tell the resident you have other residents to care for
   b. Take the call signal and place it out of reach
   c. Report this behavior to the doctor
   d. Spend extra time with the resident and realize the resident may be afraid

8. Select the appropriate room lighting for the terminally ill resident.
   a. Well lighted
   b. Dim lighting
   c. Semidark
   d. Dark

9. Which one of the following senses is the last to leave in the dying resident?
   a. Smell
   b. Hearing
   c. Speech
   d. Vision

10. How often should the nurse assistant give oral hygiene to the dying resident?
    a. Every 2 hours and as needed
    b. Every 3 hours
    c. Every 4 hours
    d. Every 30 minutes

11. Select the appropriate response if the dying resident's throat has excessive mucus.
    a. Suction the resident gently
    b. Change the tube and suction for 1 minute
    c. Ask another nurse assistant to suction the resident
    d. Report the information to the charge nurse

12. Select the appropriate response if the family of a dying resident requests to spend the day with the resident.
    a. Tell the family they may visit for 2 hours only
    b. Tell the family the visiting hours are from 8:00 A.M. to 8:00 P.M.
    c. Tell the family they can't visit all day
    d. Tell the family they may visit as long as desired

13. Select the appropriate response if a family member ask, "What did the doctor say about the lab work?"
    a. Check the chart and give the family the results
    b. Ignore the question
    c. Tell the family you have no idea
    d. Refer the family to the charge nurse

14. Select the appropriate action by the nurse assistant if the resident requires care while the family members are visiting.
    a. Perform the care with the family in the room.
    b. Ask the family if they would like to assist with the care.
    c. Ask the family to leave and return when the care is completed.
    d. Wait until the family members leave.

15. All of the following are methods for dealing with tearful family members EXCEPT:
    a. Ask the family members if they would like to talk to someone
    b. Pretend you don't see the family member crying
    c. Give the family member a tissue
    d. Support the family member and listen if they want to talk

16. Select the appropriate response if a family member expresses confusion about the resident's terminal illness.
    a. Refuse to discuss the resident's condition
    b. Explain in detail the resident's condition
    c. Ask the family, "What's confusing about death?"
    d. Refer the family member to the charge nurse

17. Which one of the following procedures would assist in relaxing a restless terminal resident?
    a. Repositioning every 3 hours
    b. Repositioning every 2 hours along with a back rub
    c. Oral hygiene and repositioning every 4 hours
    d. Repositioning every 2 hours, oral hygiene, and a back rub

18. Repositioning the terminal resident will aid in preventing which of the following conditions?
    a. Decubitus
    b. Confusion
    c. Abrasions
    d. Cyanosis

19. Select the appropriate number of stages of death.
    a. Two
    b. Three
    c. Four
    d. Five

20. All of the following are stages of dying EXCEPT:
    a. Denial and depression
    b. Anger and acceptance
    c. Joy and happiness
    d. Bargaining

21. Select the stage at which the terminal resident may express unwillingness to accept his or her condition.
    a. Anger
    b. Bargaining
    c. Denial
    d. Depression

22. Select the stage at which the terminal resident may request a minister, priest, or rabbi.
    a. Denial
    b. Bargaining
    c. Depression
    d. Acceptance

23. Select the stage at which the dying resident may become quiet and withdrawn.
    a. Anger
    b. Bargaining

c. Acceptance

d. Denial

24. Select the stage the dying resident may become demanding.
    a. Anger
    b. Denial
    c. Depression
    d. Acceptance

25. Which stage would the nurse assistant understand the terminal resident is experiencing if he or she is talking about inward feelings?
    a. Bargaining
    b. Depression
    c. Acceptance
    d. Denial

26. Select the appropriate response by the nurse assistant if the dying resident requests spiritual guidance.
    a. Call the priest
    b. Call the rabbi
    c. Notify the charge nurse
    d. Call the minister

27. Select the appropriate description regarding a dying resident's pain level.
    a. Little or no pain
    b. Excessive pain
    c. Moderate pain
    d. Constant pain

28. A common complaint of the dying resident is which one of the following?
    a. Complaint of feeling warm
    b. Complaint of feeling cold
    c. Complaint of dizziness
    d. Complaint of itching

29. All of the following characterize the pulse of a dying resident EXCEPT:
    a. Fast
    b. Weak
    c. Slow
    d. Irregular

30. A death rattle is best described as:
    a. Hiccups
    b. Mucus in the respiratory tract

c. Wheezing

d. Excessive coughing

31. Which one of the following blood pressures would indicate that the terminal resident is approaching death?
    a. 140/90
    b. 100/60
    c. 120/50
    d. 80/50

32. All of the following are characteristic of a dying resident's respiratory rate EXCEPT:
    a. Slow
    b. Irregular
    c. Fast
    d. Difficult

33. Which one of the following codes indicates that a resident has stopped breathing?
    a. Code red
    b. Code blue
    c. Code orange
    d. Code yellow

34. Postmortem care is best described as:
    a. Care before death
    b. Comfort measures
    c. Care after death
    d. Care during the dying process

35. All of the following are included in postmortem care EXCEPT:
    a. Leaving the eyes open
    b. Personal care
    c. Placing a shroud over the body
    d. Labeling the body

36. Select the appropriate action of the nurse assistant regarding a deceased resident's dentures.
    a. Place in a denture cup with water
    b. Place in the resident's mouth
    c. Remove the dentures and place in an empty denture cup
    d. Give the dentures to the family

37. In which one of the following positions is the deceased resident placed?
    a. High Fowler's
    b. Right Sim's

c. Supine
d. Prone

38. All of the following terms refer to death EXCEPT:
   a. Expired
   b. Deceased
   c. Lifeless
   d. Vital

39. Rigor mortis is best described as:
   a. Softening of the body after death
   b. Stiffening of the body after death
   c. Uncontrolled movements after death
   d. The release of bodily secretions

40. A deceased resident's body is prepared and sent to which area in the hospital?
   a. Lab
   b. X-ray department
   c. Environmental services
   d. Morgue

Answers

1. a. A terminal condition is a disease or condition with no medical cure, and is likely to cause death.

2. d. Ask the resident if he or she would like to speak to the charge nurse.

3. a. Hospice is professional nursing care in the home for terminal residents.

4. a. Emotional support, medical care, and comfort measures for the terminal residents and their family members are the primary purposes of hospice care.

5. d. Hospice services are available 24 hours a day for the terminally ill resident.

6. b. Listen and allow the resident to express his or her feelings.

7. d. Spend extra time with the resident and realize the resident may be afraid.

8. a. The terminally ill resident's room should be well lighted.

9. b. Hearing is the last sense to leave the dying resident.

10. a. The dying resident should have oral hygiene at least every two hours and whenever necessary. The oral cavity may become dry due to mouth breathing and the presence of a nasogastric tube or nasogastric oxygen.

11. d. Report excessive mucus in the throat and allow the charge nurse to suction the resident.

12. d. Tell the family they may visit as long as desired.

13. d. The nurse assistant should never discuss information regarding diagnosis, prognosis, or lab values with the family members. Always refer the family to the charge nurse.

14. b. Ask the family if they would like to assist with the care. Residents and family members are encouraged to participate in the care as much as they feel comfortable with and are capable of doing.

15. b. Never ignore the crying family member; be supportive, offer tissues, listen, and encourage the family members to speak with social services.

16. d. Refer the family member to the charge nurse.

17. d. Comfort and relaxing measures would be repositioning every 2 hours, oral hygiene, and a back rub.

18. a. Frequent turning or repositioning will assist in preventing decubitus.

19. d. The dying resident experiences five stages of death: denial, depression, anger, bargaining, and acceptance.

20. c. Denial, depression, anger, bargaining and acceptance are the five stages of death. Joy and happiness are not listed in the five stages.

21. c. Unwillingness to accept the terminal condition is experienced in the denial stage.

22. b. At the bargaining stage the resident may request spiritual guidance.

23. c. The dying resident may become quiet and withdrawn during the acceptance stage.

24. a. At the anger stage of dying the resident is likely to become demanding.

25. b. Inward feelings are likely to be expressed during the depression stage of dying.

26. c. Notify the charge nurse if the dying resident requests spiritual guidance.

27. a. The dying resident may experience little or no pain due to the decreased blood flow to the brain. However, some residents may experience pain.

28. b. A common complaint of the dying resident is feeling cold.

29. c. The pulse of a dying resident is fast and becomes weak and irregular.

30. b. A death rattle is mucus in the respiratory tract heard during the breathing process.

31. d. The blood pressure decreases before death.

32. c. The dying resident's respiratory rate is slow, irregular, and difficult.

33. b. A code blue is generally the code for respiratory arrest. Review the codes of the facility in which you are working.

34. c. Providing care to the deceased resident is postmortem care.

35. a. Postmortem care consists of personal care, closing the eyes, putting dentures in the mouth, folding the arms over the abdomen, placing shroud over the body, and labeling the body.

36. b. The deceased resident's dentures should be placed in the mouth before rigor mortis begins.

37. c. The deceased resident is positioned in a supine position.

38. d. Expired, deceased, and lifeless are terms that refer to death. Vital refers to life.

39. b. Rigor mortis is stiffening of the body after death.

40. d. The deceased resident's body is prepared and sent to the morgue.

14

Home Health Care

DIRECTIONS: Each question contains four suggested responses. Select the one best response to each question.

ANSWERS: See answers at the end of the questions.

1. Home health care is best described as:
   a. Medical care by telephone in the home
   b. Professional, supervised, individualized medical care in the home
   c. Daily home visits by the physician in the home
   d. Out-patient treatment in the clinic

2. All of the following conditions will qualify the resident for home health services EXCEPT:
   a. Recent hospitalization
   b. Recent surgery
   c. Recent CVA with weakness
   d. Loneliness

3. All of the following are purposes for home health care EXCEPT:
   a. Monitoring in-home care until the resident is stable
   b. Teaching the resident to care for himself or herself
   c. Providing individualized therapy
   d. Assisting the resident to become dependent

4. Select the state requirement to perform as a home health aide.
   a. Completion of an approved nurse assistant program
   b. Completion of an approved home health aide program
   c. On-the-job-training in a home health agency
   d. Successful completion of a state home health examination

5. Select the initial response of the home health aide prior to the first home visit.
   a. Notify the hospital for a copy of the discharge summary
   b. Review the resident's chart and assignment sheet
   c. Notify the resident and ask about his or her condition

   d. Notify the doctor for the care necessary

6. Which team member supervises the home health aide in the home?
   a. Registered nurse (RN)
   b. Doctor
   c. Licensed vocation nurse (LVN)
   d. Certified nurse assistant (CNA)

7. Which one of the following is necessary prior to admission to home health services?
   a. Family consent
   b. Bank account
   c. Physician's order
   d. Terminal diagnosis

8. Select the appropriate difference between hospital care and home health care for the home assistant.
   a. Works in the home with the registered nurse
   b. Works in the home with the licensed vocational nurse
   c. Works alone in the home and notifies the supervisor via telephone
   d. Works directly with the physician in the home

9. Select the responsibility of the home health aide in the home.
   a. To assist with activities of daily living
   b. To change the resident's surgical dressing
   c. To assist with muscle strengthening and ambulation
   d. To give emotional support only

10. Which response is appropriate if the homebound resident refuses the home health aide's services?
    a. Force the resident to receive services and report to supervisor.
    b. Report to the supervisor.
    c. Try encouraging the resident; if this is not effective, report to the supervisor.
    d. Document the care that was given.

11. Assignment sheets are completed by which team member?
    a. Physician

b. Supervisor

c. Registered nurse

d. Home health aide

12. All of the following are appropriate responses of the home health aide regarding in-home medication EXCEPT:

a. Administering the resident's medications

b. Reminding the resident of medication time

c. Reading the labels on the medication bottles

d. Assisting the resident with the correct dosage

13. Which information should be documented if the resident has periods of forgetfulness and is disoriented?

a. Mental status is disoriented

b. Resident is unable to remember eating lunch and room location

c. Resident is alert and oriented

d. Resident has periods of being disoriented

14. Select the appropriate action of the home health aide regarding soiled linen on the resident's bed.

a. Remove the linen and place in the linen hamper.

b. Remove the linen, wash and dry the linen.

c. Pad the soiled area with a sheet.

d. Allow a family member to change the linen.

15. Which action by the home health aide would indicate ethical behavior?

a. Administering a pain tablet for pain

b. Leaving the assignment sheet in the office

c. Notifying the resident prior to the visit

d. Arriving 2 hours late to give care

16. Select the appropriate term for refusing to give a neighbor important medical information regarding the home care resident.

a. Confidentiality

b. Accuracy

c. Rudeness

d. Inconsiderateness

17. Select the appropriate set of vital signs that require immediate reporting.

a. B/P 130/80 - 99.6-72-18

b. B/P 140/90 - 99-78-16

c. B/P 128/78 - 101-80-20

d. B/P 120/80 - 98.6-80-18

18. A frayed wire is observed on the home care resident's toaster. Select the appropriate action of the home health aide.

a. Allow the resident to continue using the toaster

b. Reposition the toaster with the frayed wire away from the resident

c. Ignore the wire and realize that this is not a problem

d. Discourage use until the wire is repaired

19. Which nursing task is the home health aide not permitted to carry out?

a. Light meal preparation

b. Changing a sterile dressing

c. Transportation to the doctor

d. Light housekeeping

20. Tracheostomy care is performed by which home health team member?

a. Physician

b. Licensed nurse

c. Physical therapist

d. Home health aide

21. Catheterization is best described as:

a. Sterile procedure performed by licensed nurses

b. Sterile procedure performed by home heath aides

c. Sterile procedure performed by the physician

d. Sterile procedure performed by the caregiver

22. Transcultural is best described as rreferring to all of the following EXCEPT:

a. Various beliefs and options

b. Different lifestyles

c. Varying customs from resident to resident

d. Same experiences for every resident

23. All of the following are in-home safety measures EXCEPT:
    a. Removing spills
    b. Burning candles for light
    c. Removing clutter from the floor
    d. Never overloading electrical outlets

24. Select the appropriate light meal for the home health resident with hypertension.
    a. Ham sandwich, french fries, and milk
    b. Pizza and Coke
    c. Bland chicken sandwich, fresh fruit, juice, and coffee
    d. Tuna sandwich, potato chips, and juice

25. Select the appropriate light meal for the home health resident with diabetes.
    a. Spaghetti, salad, garlic bread, apple pie, and milk
    b. Hamburger, fries, and a large Coke
    c. Fried chicken, mashed potatoes, and a strawberry malt
    d. Baked chicken, vegetables, salad, fresh fruit, and a diet drink

26. Select the appropriate response if the resident requests items from the grocery store.
    a. Tell the resident yes
    b. Tell the resident you can't
    c. Tell the resident not today
    d. Explain that you are not allowed to grocery shop

27. A family member requests permission to administer the resident's insulin. Select the appropriate response.
    a. Allow the family member to give the insulin
    b. Tell the family member they should not
    c. Ask the family member to call the supervisor
    d. Notify the supervisor to schedule diabetic care teaching

28. Select the appropriate location for emergency numbers.
    a. Beside the television
    b. Attached to the refrigerator
    c. Next to the telephone
    d. In the den area

29. A resident is found unconscious in the home. Select the appropriate initial response by the home health aide.
    a. Notify 911
    b. Notify the supervisor
    c. Notify the doctor
    d. Notify family members

30. Select the appropriate action by the home health aide if a family member involves you in a family dispute.
    a. Agree with the family members
    b. Remain nonjudgmental
    c. Agree with the resident
    d. Offer your opinions

31. All of the following are methods of infection control in the home EXCEPT:
    a. Dusting the furniture
    b. Personal care
    c. Washing dishes in cold water
    d. Washing soiled linen

32. All of the following are performed prior to providing home care EXCEPT:
    a. Identifying the resident
    b. Explanation of the procedure
    c. Hand washing
    d. Notification of the supervisor

33. Select the appropriate action of the home health aide after completion of the home visit.
    a. Document care given and tolerance in pocket notebook
    b. Report care given to the resident
    c. The care given is documented on the nurse assistant's note
    d. Notify the supervisor

34. How often is the home health aide supervised in the home?
    a. Once a month
    b. Twice a month
    c. Three times a month
    d. Four times a month

35. Which form is completed to verify conversations with the supervisor or office staff?
    a. A home visit form
    b. Mileage form

c. Telephone communication form

d. No specific form required

36. Which form is completed and left in the office to indicate daily activity?

   a. Nurse's note form

   b. Route slip

   c. Face sheet

   d. Mileage form

37. Select the appropriate method of calculating daily mileage.

   a. Set the odometer from your house to the office

   b. Estimate mileage according to the Thomas map

   c. Mileage is not reimbursed

   d. Set the odometer from the office to the first resident's house

38. Select the appropriate method to calculate the rate of mileage reimbursement.

   a. Calculate 10 miles per visit and multiply by .20 (20 cents).

b. Estimate a standard mileage reimbursement of 25 cents a mile.

c. Follow the polices and procedures of the home health agency.

d. Calculate $2.00 per resident per day.

39. Select the appropriate charting time frames after completing home visit.

   a. After each visit

   b. Weekly

   c. Every other visit

   d. End of the day

40. Which team member completes the discharge summary sheet?

   a. Licensed vocational nurse

   b. Registered nurse

   c. Home health assistants

   d. Director of nurses

Answers

1. b. Home health care is professional, supervised, individual care in the home.

2. d. The resident must have a medical condition requiring monitoring or medication.

3. d. Home health services assist the resident to become independent, never dependent.

4. b. To qualify as a home health aide according to state requirements, you must complete an approved home health aide program.

5. b. The home health aide must review the fact sheet and health record and follow the assignment sheet or treatment plan.

6. a. The registered nurse (RN) supervises the home health aide.

7. c. A physician's order is necessary prior to admission. The family is included in the resident's plan of care.

8. c. The nurse assistant works in the hospital under the direct supervision of licensed nurses; in home care the home health aide works alone and notifies the supervisor by telephone if any problems are observed.

9. a. The responsibility of the home health aide is to assist the resident with bathing, grooming, and nutrition, which are called activity of daily living skills. Light housekeeping is also required.

10. c. Try encouraging the resident; if unsuccessful, notify the supervisor.

11. b. The registered nurse completes the assignment sheet.

12. a. Administering medication is not the responsibility of the home health aide.

13. b. The resident is unable to remember eating lunch, and room location.

14. b. Remove the linen, wash and dry it.

15. c. Ethical behavior for a home health aide includes notification prior to arriving at the resident's home.

16. a. Confidentiality means keeping the resident's medical information private.

17. c. Elevated temperatures should be reported immediately. Elevation usually indicates infections.

18. d. Discourage use until the toaster wire can be repaired.

19. b. The home health aide is not permitted to change a sterile dressing.

20. b. The licensed nurse performs tracheostomy care.

21. a. Catheterization is a sterile procedure performed by licensed nurses.

22. d. Transcultural refers to individual differences, lifestyles, cultures, beliefs, and religious fellowships.

23. b. In-home safety measures would be removing spills and clutter from the floor and never overloading electrical outlets.

24. c. Bland chicken sandwich, fresh fruit, juice, and coffee is a diet with low or no sodium.

25. d. Baked chicken, vegetables, salad, fresh fruit, and a diet drink is a light meal for a diabetic resident, consisting of foods with low or no sugars.

26. a. Grocery shopping as needed is a part of the home health aide's responsibility.

27. d. A family member can administer the resident's medication. Notify the supervisor, and the family member can be scheduled for instruction in medication administering.

28. c. Emergency telephone numbers should be posted next to the telephone.

29. a. Notify 911 in case of any emergency involving resident's health.

30. b. A nonjudgmental attitude should be developed when dealing with residents and family members.

31. c. Dishes should be washed in a detergent and hot water to cleanse the dishes and promote infection control.

32. d. Prior to performing care in the home, the home health aide should identify the resident, explain the procedure, and wash his or her hands. Notifying the supervisor is not necessary unless there is a problem.

33. c. Upon completion of a home visit, the care given is documented on the nurse assistant's note.

34. a. A supervised home health aide visit is performed once a month.

35. c. A telephone communication form is completed to keep an accurate record of conversations with the office staff.

36. b. A route slip or daily activity log lists each resident and tentative time of visit.

37. d. Mileage is calculated from the office to the first resident's house.

38. c. Obtain the mileage rate and calculation procedure through the agencies polices and procedures. The amount and procedure can vary from agency to agency.

39. a. Charting is completed after each visit to ensure accuracy.

40. b. The registered nurse completes the discharge summary sheet and supervises the resident's discharge from the agency.

Part Two:

Basic Nursing Procedures

with

Questions and Answers

15

Infection Control: Handwashing Procedure

HANDWASHING PROCEDURE

Remember to use a clean paper towel to turn on the faucet.

Also remember to shut off the faucet with a clean paper towel after completing the handwashing procedure.

Proper handwashing prevents the spread of germs.

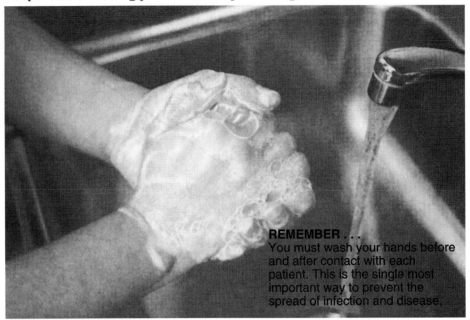

REMEMBER . . .
You must wash your hands before and after contact with each patient. This is the single most important way to prevent the spread of infection and disease.

1. When using bar soap be sure to rinse the soap before use.

2. Wash your hands for 1 to 2 minutes.

3. Use friction.

4. Wash 2 inches above the wrist.

5. Clean under the nails.

6. Hold your hands lower than your elbow.

7. Rinse well.

8. Dry the hands thoroughly.

9. Shut off the faucet with a clean paper towel.

QUESTIONS

DIRECTIONS: Each question contains four suggested responses. Select the one best response to each question.

ANSWERS: See answers at the end of the section.

1. All of the following are purposes for handwashing EXCEPT:
   a. Prevent the spread of infections
   b. Remove microorganisms from the hands
   c. Prevent cross contamination
   d. Sterilize the hands

2. Select the appropriate infection control method to use before and after a resident's care.
   a. Disinfectant
   b. Sterilization
   c. Handwashing
   d. Wearing a gown

3. Which one of the following is the length of time necessary to thoroughly wash the hands.
   a. 1 to 2 minutes
   b. 3 to 4 minutes
   c. 5 to 6 minutes
   d. 7 to 8 minutes

4. Select the appropriate action of the nurse assistant when bar soap is used for handwashing.
   a. Wipe the soap with a paper towel.
   b. Wash the hands an additional minute.
   c. Leave the soap in a small amount of water.
   d. Rinse the soap before use.

5. Which one of the following actions should the nurse assistant perform prior to handwashing?
   a. Turn the faucet on without a paper towel.
   b. Use a paper towel to turn on the faucet.
   c. Use friction between the fingers.
   d. Scrub in a rotating motion.

6. Select the appropriate hand position during handwashing.
   a. Even with the elbow.
   b. Higher than the elbow.
   c. Lower than the elbow.
   d. Higher and lower than the elbow.

7. Select the appropriate level to wash above the wrist.
   a. 2 inches
   b. 4 inches
   c. 5 inches
   d. 6 inches

8. Effective handwashing requires all of the following EXCEPT:
   a. Enough soap to produce a lather
   b. Friction—rubbing skin against skin
   c. Circular scrubbing motion
   d. Small amount of running water

9. Select the appropriate action of the nurse assistant if the hands accidentally touch the inside of the sink during the handwashing procedure.
   a. Use an additional paper towel to dry well.
   b. Rinse the hands an additional minute.
   c. Repeat the handwashing process.
   d. Don't worry; the sink is clean.

10. After washing your hands, turn the faucet off:
    a. And apply gloves
    b. Using a clean paper towel
    c. And dry hands
    d. With wet hands

Putting on isolation gown, mask, and disposable gloves and taking off soiled gloves, mask, and gown

Place gown opening toward the back.

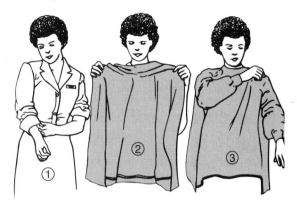

Secure the neck tie.

Be sure all clothing is covered.

1. Be sure the mask covers the nose and mouth.
2. Apply the gloves over the cuffs of the gown.

Removal of Gown, Gloves, and Mask

3. Remove the gloves and wash your hands.
4. Remove the gown and wash your hands.
5. Remove the mask and wash your hands.

11. In which one of the following areas should the nurse assistant put on the isolation garments?

    a. Utility room

    b. Nurse's lounge

    c. Inside the resident's room

    d. Outside the resident's room

12. All of the following are methods used to apply the isolation gown EXCEPT:

    a. Place the gown opening toward the back.

    b. Tie the gown at the neck.

    c. Place the opening toward the front.

    d. Tie the gown at the waist.

13. Which one of the following isolation items are put on after the gown?

    a. Gloves

    b. Mask

    c. Shoes

    d. Hat

14. Select the appropriate method of putting on the isolation mask.

    a. Place the mask over the nose only.

    b. Place the mask over the nose and mouth.

    c. Cover the nose and mouth and tie the top strings.

    d. Cover the nose and mouth and tie the top and bottom strings.

15. Which statement should the nurse assistant understand regarding applying gloves for care of the isolation resident.

    a. Gloves are to cover gown cuffs.

    b. Gloves are to be applied before the gown.

    c. Gloves should not cover gown cuffs.

    d. Gloves are optional with gown and mask.

16. All of the following are methods to remove isolation garments EXCEPT:

    a. Remove all items inside the isolation room.

    b. Remove gloves first and then wash your hands.

    c. Remove the mask first.

    d. Remove gloves, gown, and mask.

17. Select the appropriate responsibility of the nurse assistant after removing the isolation garments.

    a. Exit the room and wash hands in the utility room.

    b. Wash hands in the isolation room.

    c. Report to the charge nurse and wash hands at the nurses' station.

    d. Wash hands in the employee lounge area.

18. Isolation is best described as:

    a. Protection of the resident

    b. Protection of the staff

    c. Protection of the residents and staff

    d. Allowing the resident privacy

19. All of the following are rules for the resident in isolation EXCEPT:

    a. Door is kept closed.

    b. Disposable eating utensils are used.

    c. Double bagging is required.

    d. Door can be left open.

20. Select the appropriate method to remove soiled linen and trash from the isolation room.

    a. Tie the bags tightly and place outside the door.

    b. Double bag inside the room and place outside the door.

    c. Tie both containers tightly and carry to the utility room.

    d. Tie tightly: double bag outside the room with the help of a coworker.

Answers

1. d. The hands are washed clean but not sterilized during the handwashing process.

2. c. Handwashing is performed before and after residents care. The nurse assistant should remember to wash his or her hands between care of residents, after using the bathroom, after sneezing or coughing, and whenever his or her hands come in contact with a contaminated surface.

3. a. The hands should be washed for 1 to 2 minutes for thorough cleaning.

4. d. Bar soaps should be rinsed thoroughly before use.

5. b. The faucet should be turned on with a paper towel, since germs can be found on the faucet.

6. c. The hands should be held below the level of the elbow. Holding the hands down will prevent contamination of the washed area.

7. a. The hands should be washed 2 inches above the wrist.

8. d. The water should be continuous with enough force to assist in removing the soap.

9. c. The handwashing procedure must be repeated if the sink is touched with the clean hands, they are now considered to be contaminated.

10. b. The faucet is shut off with a paper towel to prevent contaminating the clean hands.

11. d. The isolation garments should be put on outside the resident's room.

12. c. The isolation gown is put on with the opening toward the back and tied at the neck and waist to cover clothing.

13. b. The mask is applied after the application of the gown.

14. d. The mask should cover the nose and mouth with the top and bottom string tied.

15. a. The nurse assistant should cover gown cuffs with gloves that are applied after the gown and mask are put on.

16. c. Never remove the mask first. The sequence for removing the isolation garments is gloves, gown, and mask.

17. b. The responsibility of the nurse assistant after removing gloves, mask, and gown is handwashing inside the room.

18. c. Isolation is protecting the resident from other organisms in the hospital setting. Staff members must also protect themselves from contracting the resident's infectious disease by wearing isolation clothing.

19. d. Rules for the resident in isolation are using disposable eating utensils, keeping the room door closed, having linen and trash hampers inside the room, and double bagging at the end of the nurse assistant's shift.

20. d. The linen and trash from the isolation room should be tied tightly inside the room, and a coworker should hold another red bag outside the door for double bagging.

16

Bedmaking Procedure

Types of Bedmaking

1. Closed bed
2. Open bed
3. Occupied bed
4. Postoperative bed

CLOSED BED

The bed is clean and ready for an admission.

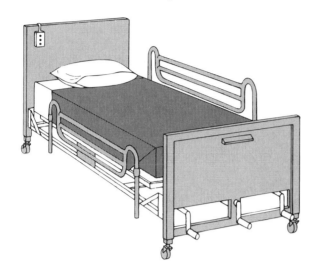

OCCUPIED BED

Linen is changed with the resident in the bed.

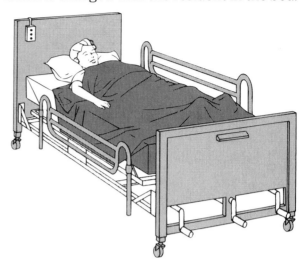

OPEN BED

Assigned to a resident.

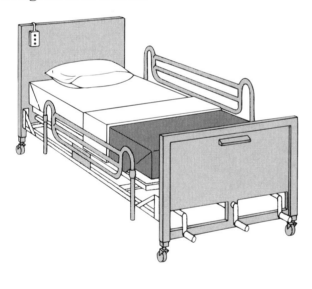

POSTOPERATIVE BED

Awaiting the resident returning from surgery.

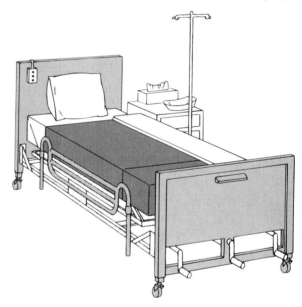

TRIANGULAR OR MITERED CORNERS

Assists the sheet to stay in place

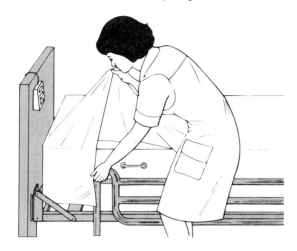

Complete Triangle Corner

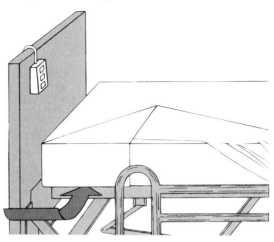

Tuck the sheet under the mattress

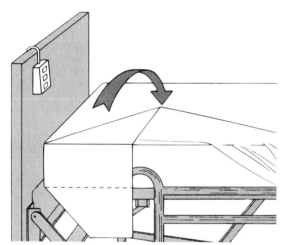

- Make sure resident is comfortable.
- Raise the bedside rails for safety.

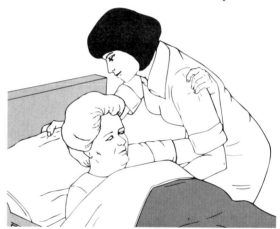

QUESTIONS

DIRECTIONS: Each question contains four suggested responses. Select the one best response to each question.

ANSWERS: See answers at the end of the questions.

1. Select the appropriate linen set for bedmaking.
   a. One sheet, draw sheet, blanket, pillowcase, and spread
   b. Two sheets, two draw sheets, blanket, and spread
   c. Blanket, spread, two sheets, one draw sheet, and pillowcase
   d. Pillowcase, two draw sheets, blanket, and spread

2. Select the appropriate order in which linen is placed in the chair before bedmaking.
   a. Pillowcase, bottom sheet, draw sheet, sheet, blanket, and spread
   b. Pillowcase, blanket, sheets, draw sheet, and spread
   c. Bottom sheet, draw sheet, sheet, blanket, spread, and pillowcase
   d. Draw sheet, bottom sheet, sheet, blanket, spread, and pillowcase

3. Which one of the following items of linen should be wrinkle free during bedmaking?
   a. Top sheet
   b. Bottom sheet
   c. Blanket
   d. Spread

4. Select the correct position of the bed during bedmaking.
   a. Slightly elevated
   b. Highest position
   c. Lowest position
   d. Comfortable according to the individual

5. All of the following are methods of placing the bottom sheet on the mattress EXCEPT:
   a. Fold the bottom sheet lengthwise on the mattress.
   b. Place the centerfold of the sheet in the center of the mattress.
   c. Shake the sheet freely and center on the mattress.
   d. Place the large hem to the head of the bed.

6. Mitered corner is best described as:
   a. A method to keep the sheet tight on the bed
   b. A method to keep the draw sheet from wrinkling
   c. A method to keep the covers off the feet
   d. A method to keep the mattress from sliding

7. Which one of the following linen pieces is placed next to the bottom sheet?
   a. Cloth draw sheet
   b. Rubber draw sheet
   c. Top sheet
   d. Blanket

8. Select the appropriate action of the nurse assistant if the clean linen accidentally touches the floor.
   a. Place the contaminated area away from the resident.
   b. Shake the linen to remove any particles.
   c. Realize the floor is cleaned daily.
   d. Replace the contaminated linen.

9. In which position is the pillow placed after the bedmaking procedure?
   a. Foot of the bed with the open side facing the door
   b. Head of the bed with the open side facing the door
   c. Head of the bed with the open side away from the door
   d. On the chair next to the bed

10. Which one of the following is the last action of the nurse assistant after completion of the bedmaking procedure?
    a. Opening the privacy curtain
    b. Attach the call signal to the bed
    c. Reposition the bed
    d. Handwashing

Answers
1. c. The appropriate linen set for bedmaking is two sheets, one draw sheet, blanket, spread, and pillowcase.

2. c. The linen is placed on the bedside chair according to the order the linen is being placed on the bed: the bottom sheet on top, followed by the draw sheet, top sheet, blanket, spread, and pillowcase.

3. b. The bottom sheet should be wrinkle free to prevent decubitus.

4. d. The bed should be at a comfortable working height. Remember, the heights may vary according to the height of the nurse assistant.

5. c. Never shake the linen during bedmaking, shaking increases organisms in the air.

6. a. Using mitered corners is a method to keep the sheets tight on the bed.

7. b. The rubber draw sheet is placed on top of the bottom sheet to protect from soilage.

8. d. The linen is contaminated if it comes in contact with the floor and must be replaced.

9. c. The position of the pillow is at the head of the bed with open side away from the door.

10. d. Handwashing is the last action of the nurse assistant after completion of the bedmaking procedure.

17

Personal Care Procedures

1. Oral hygiene
2. Bathing
3. Back rub
4. Shaving
5. Nail care
6. Combing the hair

Oral hygiene to the unconscious resident

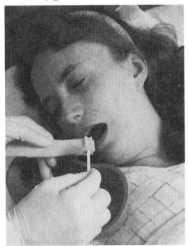

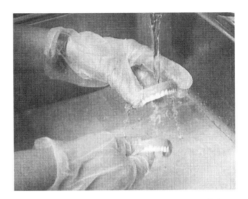

Cleanse the dentures thoroughly with cool running water.

Always wear gloves.

Use cool water.

Position the head to the side.

1. Wash your hands.

2. Greet the resident.

3. Check the resident's armband.

4. Assemble your equipment—towel, gloves, tongue depressor, emesis basin, and oral glycerine swabs.

5. Clean all parts of the mouth, tongue, palate, and teeth.

6. Be aware of privacy, safety, communications, infection control, independence, and dignity.

7. Wash your hands.

8. Record and report observations to the charge nurse.

1. Wash your hands before and after the procedure.

2. Greet the resident.

3. Check the armband.

4. Explain the procedure.

5. Assemble your equipment—emesis basin; large towel; denture cup; toothbrush; toothpaste, or denture cream; mouthwash; and glycerine swabs.

6. Line the sink with a towel or water to prevent breakage.

7. Secure the resident.

8. Place the call signal in reach.

9. Record and report observations to the charge nurse.

DIRECTIONS: Each question contains four suggested responses. Select the one best response to each question.

ANSWERS: See answers at the end of the questions.

1. Oral hygiene is best described as:
   a. Cleaning the body parts
   b. Removing facial hair
   c. Cleansing the mouth
   d. Nail care

2. Select the first action of the nurse assistant immediately before performing oral hygiene.
   a. Check the armband
   b. Assemble equipment
   c. Explain the procedure
   d. Wash your hands

3. Infection control can be promoted during oral hygiene by which action of the nurse assistant?
   a. Draping the resident
   b. Diluting the mouthwash
   c. Washing the hands
   d. Wearing gloves

4. Select the appropriate condition of a resident to receive oral hygiene with a tongue depressor and oral glycerine swabs.
   a. Ambulatory
   b. Incontinent
   c. Unconscious
   d. Conscious

5. Which complication is prevented by placing the unconscious resident's head to the side during oral hygiene?
   a. Choking
   b. Dizziness
   c. Tongue bite
   d. Shortness of breath

6. Select the appropriate action of the nurse assistant to prevent breakage of the dentures.
   a. Rinse the dentures inside a denture cup.
   b. Line the sink with a paper towel or water.
   c. Rise the dentures inside an emesis basin.
   d. Brush the dentures inside the mouth.

7. Select the appropriate water temperature to rinse the dentures.
   a. Cold
   b. Warm
   c. Semi-hot
   d. Hot

8. All of the following oral hygiene observations are reported EXCEPT:
   a. Dry, cracked tongue
   b. Coated white tongue
   c. Sores
   d. White teeth

9. Which action would promote the resident's independence during the oral hygiene procedure?
   a. Allowing the resident to assist
   b. Performing oral hygiene for the resident
   c. Requesting a family member to perform procedure
   d. Discouraging the resident's assistance

10. All of the following are actions of the nurse assistant after oral hygiene EXCEPT:
    a. Reporting any abnormalities
    b. Recording the resident's tolerance
    c. Handwashing
    d. Documentation the following day

COMPLETE BED BATH PROCEDURE

BED BATH PROCEDURE

How to use the towel as a mitten.

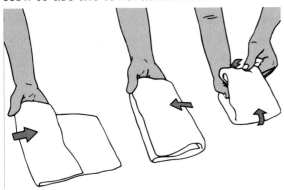

1. Wash your hands before and after the procedure.

2. Greet the resident.

3. Check the armband.

4. Explain the procedure.

5. Assemble your equipment—bath blanket, wash basin with water temperature at 115°F, towels, wash cloth, soap, gloves, and clean gown.

6. Provide privacy.

7. Provide safety.

8. Bathe the resident. Wash the face first and then the arms, chest, abdomen, legs, back, and perineal area.

9. Be sure to observe the resident's skin.

10. Secure the resident.

11. Place the call signal within reach.

12. Record and report observations to the charge nurse.

GIVING A BED BATH

Wash the face first

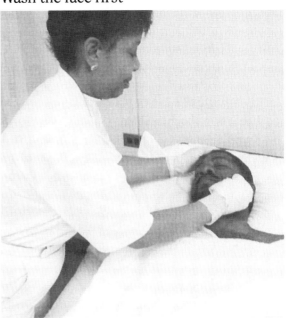

GIVING A BED BATH

Use long strokes during the bed bath

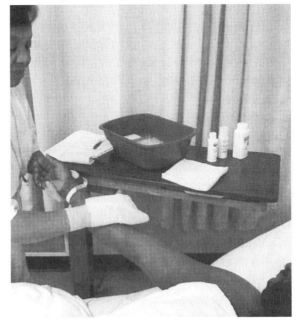

GIVING A BED BATH

Wash the legs and soak the feet in the wash basin

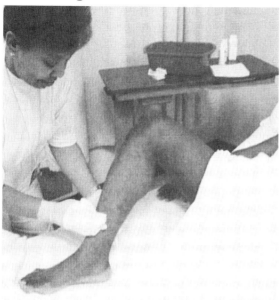

Be sure to wash the back and perineal area

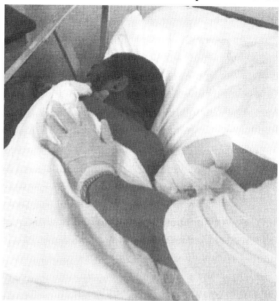

QUESTIONS ···

DIRECTIONS: Each question contains suggested responses. Select the one best response to each question.
ANSWERS: See answers at the end of the chapter.

11. Select the *first* action of the nurse assistant prior to performing a complete bed bath.
    a. Handwashing
    b. Providing privacy
    c. Explaining the procedure
    d. Assembling the equipment

12. Which one of the following health care providers should ask visitors to leave the room prior to the bed bath?
    a. Team leader
    b. Charge nurse
    c. Nurse assistant
    d. Supervisor

13. Which one of the following linen is removed prior to the bed bath?
    a. Top and bottom sheet
    b. Spread, blanket, and top sheet
    c. Blanket, spread, and bottom sheet
    d. Draw sheet, top sheet, and blanket

14. Select the appropriate water temperature for a bed bath.
    a. 105°F
    b. 110°F
    c. 115°F
    d. 120°F

15. Which body area should the nurse assistant wash first during the bed bath procedure?
    a. Hands
    b. Neck
    c. Ears
    d. Face

16. How often should the bath water be changed during the complete bed bath?
    a. After washing the anterior upper body
    b. After washing the perineal area
    c. After washing the posterior upper back
    d. After washing the legs and feet

17. Select the appropriate time during the bed bath when the nurse assistant should give the resident a back rub.
    a. After washing the perineal area
    b. Before washing the perineal area

c. After washing the feet

d. After completing the bed bath

18. To which one of the following staff members should the nurse assistant report abnormal observations during the bed bath.

   a. Charge nurse

   b. Supervisor

   c. Doctor

   d. Coworker (nurse assistant)

19. During which stage of the bed bath procedure should the nurse assistant make the resident's bed?

   a. Before the bed bath

b. After washing the upper body

c. At completion of bed bath procedure

d. After washing the lower body

20. All of the following actions are performed after the bed bath EXCEPT:

   a. Open the privacy curtain

   b. Raise the side rails

   c. Record and report observations

   d. Leave the call signal hanging freely

....

TUB BATH PROCEDURE

GIVING A TUB BATH

Clean the tub before and after use.

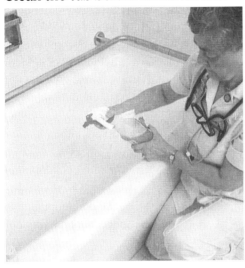

Assist the resident to wash the back.

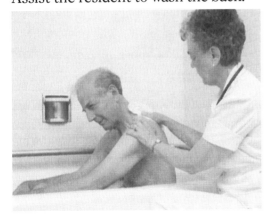

Supervise the resident closely during the bath.

1. Wash your hands before and after the procedure.

2. Greet your resident.

3. Check armband.

4. Explain the procedure.

5. Assemble equipment—bath towel, wash cloth, soap, clean clothing, and an antiseptic solution to clean the bath tub. The tub should be cleaned before and after the bath.

6. Provide privacy.

7. Provide safety—closely supervise the resident during a tub bath.

8. Allow the resident to assist, if able.

9. Record and report observations to the charge nurse.

DIRECTIONS: Each question contains four suggested responses. Select the one best response to each question.

ANSWERS: See answers at the end of the questions.

21. All of the following are purposes of the tub bath EXCEPT:
    a. Promotes relaxation
    b. Increases circulation
    c. Cleanses the skin
    d. Decreases circulation

22. Select the first action of the nurse assistant immediately before the tub bath.
    a. Assemble equipment
    b. Wash hands
    c. Check armband
    d. Provide privacy

23. Which one of the following health care workers should disinfect the tub before the tub bath?
    a. Housekeeper
    b. Nurse assistant
    c. Charge nurse
    d. Team leader

24. Select the appropriate safety precautions before the tub bath.
    a. Raise the side rail.
    b. Remove electrical appliances.
    c. Place the soap inside the tub.
    d. Completely fill the tub.

25. Which water level is appropriate for a tub bath?
    a. Fill the tub one-fourth full.
    b. Fill the tub half full.
    c. Fill the tub three-fourth full.
    d. Completely fill the tub.

26. Select the appropriate water temperature for a tub bath.
    a. 105°F
    b. 110°F
    c. 115°F
    d. 120°F

27. Which one of the following actions should the nurse assistant perform to prevent falls during the tub bath?
    a. Tell the resident to be careful.
    b. Tell the resident to use good body mechanics.
    c. Place a towel inside and outside of the tub.
    d. Leave the soap in the water.

28. All of the following are methods to prevent accidents during a tub bath EXCEPT:
    a. Place the soap in a soap dish.
    b. Fill the tub half full.
    c. Remove electrical appliances.
    d. Leave the resident unattended.

29. Which observation should the nurse assistant report immediately after the tub bath?
    a. Clear intact skin
    b. Dry skin areas
    c. Inflamed skin areas
    d. Skin softness

30. Select the appropriate information to be documented after the tub bath.
    a. Completion of tub bath, tolerance, and problems.
    b. Purpose of tub bath and time required.
    c. Length of bath and frequency of tub bath.
    d. Nurse assistant tolerance.

BACK RUB PROCEDURE

GIVING A BACK RUB

Begin at the lower back using firm, long upward strokes and circular motion around bony areas.

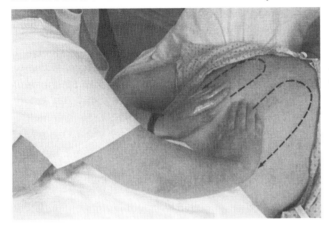

Observe the skin for abnormalities.

1. Wash your hands before and after the procedure.

2. Greet your resident.

3. Check resident's armband.

4. Explain the procedure.

5. Assemble your equipment—wash basin with warm water at 115°F, lotion, and towels.

6. Provide safety.

7. Provide privacy.

8. Offer the resident independence.

9. Place the lotion in your hands, start at the lower back, and rub toward the shoulders using a circular motion outward.

10. Observe the resident's skin.

11. Secure the resident, and place the call signal within reach.

12. Record and report observations to the charge nurse.

QUESTIONS

DIRECTIONS: Each question contains suggested responses. Select the one best response to each question.
ANSWERS: See answers at the end of the chapter.

31. A back rub is best described as:
    a. Rubbing the back with alcohol
    b. Applying lotion to the back area
    c. Rubbing the back using friction
    d. Applying an antiseptic solution to the back

32. Select the first action of the nurse assistant before giving a back rub.
    a. Explain the procedure.
    b. Wash hands.
    c. Assemble equipment.
    d. Provide privacy.

33. All of the following equipment is assembled for the back rub procedure EXCEPT:
    a. Lotion
    b. Basin of water at 115°F
    c. Towel
    d. Alcohol

34. All of the following are back rub positions EXCEPT:
    a. Supine
    b. Prone
    c. Left Sims'
    d. Right Sims'

35. Select the appropriate method to warm the lotion before the back rub.
    a. Run hot water over the lotion container in the utility room.
    b. Place the lotion in the basin of water at 115°F.

c. Warm your hands and hold the lotion container.

d. Shake the lotion for 30 seconds.

36. On which area of the back should the nurse assistant begin the back rub?
    a. Middle back
    b. Neck area
    c. Upper back
    d. Lower back

37. All of the following are rubbing methods during the back rub EXCEPT:
    a. Firm long upward strokes
    b. Short gentle upward strokes
    c. Gentle downward strokes
    d. Circular motion on bony areas

38. Select the appropriate length of time the nurse assistant should rub the resident's back.
    a. 1-1/2 to 3 minutes

b. 4 to 5 minutes
c. 6 to 7 minutes
d. 8 to 10 minutes

39. All of the following are actions of the nurse assistant after the backrub EXCEPT:
    a. Raise the side rail.
    b. Place call signal within reach.
    c. Leave the resident in a prone position.
    d. Wash your hands.

40. Which one of the following observations should be reported to the charge nurse?
    a. Clear skin
    b. Red open skin
    c. Smooth skin
    d. Warm skin

. . . .

SHAVING PROCEDURE

Shave the hair in the direction of the growth.

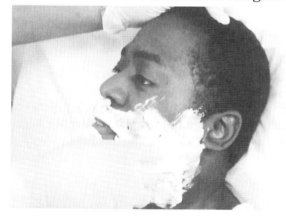

Inspect the razor before use.

Soften the beard with water before applying the shaving cream.

1. Wash your hands before and after the procedure.

2. Greet your resident.

3. Check the resident's armband.

4. Explain the procedure.

5. Assemble equipment—gloves, shaving cream, razor, aftershave lotion, towel, wash cloth, wash basin with water at 115°F, and a mirror.

6. Drape the resident; inspect the skin for moles, etc., and apply water to the beard to soften. Apply shaving cream and inspect the razor for safety; shave in the direction of the growth of the hair. Rinse the razor as needed.

7. Remove the excess shaving cream.

8. Apply the aftershave lotion.

9. Secure the resident.

10. Place the call signal within reach.

11. Record and report observations to the charge nurse.

DIRECTIONS: Each question contains four suggested responses. Select the one best response to each question.

ANSWERS: See answers at the end of the chapter.

41. All of the following equipment could be assembled for shaving EXCEPT:
    a. Basin of water at 115°F
    b. Shaving cream
    c. Safety or electrical razor
    d. Straight razor

42. Select the appropriate action of the nurse assistant before attempting to shave the resident's beard.
    a. Inspect the skin for facial moles.
    b. Wash your hands.
    c. Check the armband.
    d. Provide privacy.

43. Which one of the following methods should the nurse assistant perform to soften the beard?
    a. Comb the beard downward.
    b. Wrap hot towels around resident's face.
    c. Apply warm water to the beard with a wash cloth.
    d. Brush the beard upward.

44. Which one of the following must be used if the nurse assistant is using a safety razor?
    a. Baby oil
    b. Shaving cream
    c. Lotion
    d. Tap water

45. All of the following are actions of the nurse assistant during the shave EXCEPT:
    a. Hold the skin taut.
    b. Wear gloves.
    c. Shave in the direction of the hair growth.
    d. Rinse the razor at the completion of the shave only.

46. Select the appropriate direction the nurse assistant should give to the resident when shaving under the nose and around the mouth.
    a. Open the mouth.
    b. Keep the tongue in the hollow areas around the mouth.
    c. Close the mouth tightly.
    d. Place lips in a kissing position.

47. Select the appropriate action of the nurse assistant if the skin is accidentally nicked during the shave.
    a. Wipe the area with a towel.
    b. Apply direct pressure only.
    c. Report to the charge nurse.
    d. Apply aftershave to the area.

48. Which one of the following actions should the nurse assistant understand before shaving the resident's beard.
    a. Shaving the male resident requires a doctors order.
    b. Shaving equipment may vary per resident.
    c. Safety razor is used.
    d. Electrical razor is used.

49. Select the appropriate action of the nurse assistant to promote independence during the shave.
    a. Allow the resident to assist.
    b. Shave the resident yourself.
    c. Encourage a family member to perform the shave.
    d. Allow your coworker to perform the shave.

50. All of the following skills are performed after the shave EXCEPT:
    a. Wash hands.
    b. Place call signal within reach.
    c. Report and record information.
    d. Leave the resident in an uncomfortable position.

NAIL CARE PROCEDURE

Soak the nails before trimming.

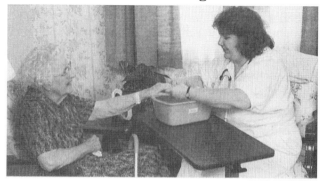

1. Wash your hands before and after the procedure.
2. Greet your resident.
3. Check the resident's armband.
4. Explain the procedure.
5. Provide privacy.
6. Provide safety.
7. Assemble equipment—emery board, orange sticks, clippers, lotion, gloves, and wash basin with water temperature at 105°.
8. Soak for approximately 5 to 10 minutes—use the orange stick to clean under the nail, clip the nail straight across, smooth the edges with the emery board, and apply lotion.
9. Secure the resident.
10. Place the call signal within reach.
11. Record and report observations to the charge nurse.

QUESTIONS

DIRECTIONS: Each question contains four suggested responses. Select the one best response to each question.

ANSWERS: See answers at the end of the chapter.

51. Select the first action of the nurse before beginning the nail care procedure.
    a. Explain the procedure.
    b. Assemble your equipment.
    c. Wash your hands.
    d. Pull the privacy curtain.

52. All of the following equipment is assembled for the nail care procedure EXCEPT:
    a. Wash basin, soap, and water at 105°F
    b. Lotion, towel, and gloves
    c. Clippers, orange stick, and emery board
    d. Scissors and alcohol

53. Which one of the following procedures should the nurse assistant perform to clean and trim the nails?
    a. Soak before cleaning and trimming.
    b. Trim the nails before soaking.
    c. Use the orange stick before soaking.
    d. Use the emery board before cleaning.

54. Select the appropriate action of the nurse assistant after soaking and cleaning the nails.
    a. Dry well and apply alcohol.
    b. Dry well and clean with the orange stick.
    c. Rinse and dry the hands.
    d. Dry well and apply lotion.

55. In which direction should the nurse assistant trim the resident's nails?
    a. Straight across
    b. Sides only
    c. V-shaped
    d. U-shaped

56. Which team member should trim the diabetic resident's nails?
    a. Doctor
    b. Nurse assistant
    c. Supervisor
    d. Charge nurse

57. Select the nail care equipment used by the nurse assistant to smooth the resident's nail edges.
    a. Scissors
    b. Emery board
    c. Electric file
    d. Sandpaper

58. Which method is used to apply lotion to the resident's hands after the nail care procedure?
    a. Gentle massage from wrist to finger tips
    b. Gentle massage beginning on the back of the hand upward
    c. Gentle massage from the finger tips toward the wrist
    d. Gentle massage beginning with palms downward

59. All of the following are performed after the nail care procedure EXCEPT:
    a. Allowing the resident to apply lotion, if able
    b. Attaching the call signal in the resident's reach
    c. Lowering the side rail
    d. Making the resident comfortable

60. Select the appropriate response by the nurse assistant if the resident's nails are too difficult to trim.
    a. Refuse to trim the nails.
    b. Report to the charge nurse.
    c. Ask a family member to trim the nails.
    d. Notify the doctor.

COMBING THE RESIDENT'S HAIR PROCEDURE

Inspect the scalp before combing the hair.

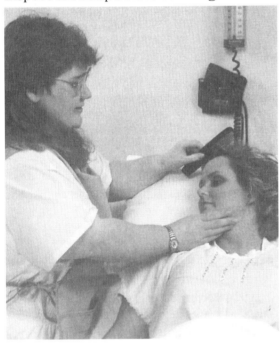

1. Wash your hands before and after the procedure.
2. Greet the resident.
3. Check the armband.
4. Explain the procedure.
5. Assemble your equipment: towel, comb, brush, gloves, and mirror.
6. Provide privacy.
7. Provide safety throughout the procedure.
8. Drape the resident and part the hair in four sections; inspect the scalp and ask the resident for his or her desired hair style.
9. Provide the resident with a mirror.
10. Secure the resident.
11. Place the call signal within reach.
12. Record and report observations to the charge nurse.

DIRECTIONS: Each question contains four suggested responses. Select the one best response to each question.

ANSWERS: See answers at the end of the questions.

61. Select the appropriate action of the nurse assistant before the hair combing procedure.
    a. Check the chart for an order.
    b. Ask the charge nurse's permission.
    c. Assemble equipment.
    d. Wash the hair.

62. All of the following equipment is used for the hair combing procedure EXCEPT:
    a. Towel
    b. Electric curlers
    c. Comb or brush
    d. Hand mirror

63. Select a safety measure used by the nurse assistant before beginning the hair combing procedure.
    a. Pulling the curtain
    b. Asking the charge nurse's permission
    c. Explanation of the procedure
    d. Identification of the resident

64. All of the following actions by the nurse assistant would promote the resident's dignity EXCEPT:
    a. Knocking before entering the room
    b. Selecting a hair style for the resident.
    c. Calling the resident by his or her name.
    d. Providing privacy.

65. Which one of the following methods should the nurse assistant perform to examine the resident's scalp?
    a. Check each hair root.
    b. Feel the scalp.

    c. Part the hair in sections.
    d. Ask the resident.

66. Which scalp observation should be reported to the charge nurse immediately?
    a. Dandruff
    b. Lice
    c. Baldness
    d. Oiliness

67. All of the following are performed during the hair combing procedure EXCEPT:
    a. Draping the resident with a towel
    b. Hair styling desirable to the nurse assistant
    c. Observation of the scalp
    d. Combing the hair in sections

68. Select the appropriate action of the nurse assistant if the resident has long hair.
    a. Suggest a hair net.
    b. Suggest a rubber band.
    c. Suggest a braid.
    d. Suggest cutting the hair.

69. Which one of the following actions should the nurse assistant perform immediately after combing the resident's hair?
    a. Open the curtain.
    b. Lower the bed.
    c. Wash the hands.
    d. Offer the resident a mirror.

70. All of the following are actions of the nurse assistant after completing the hair combing procedure EXCEPT:
    a. Opening the curtain
    b. Allowing the call signal to hang freely
    c. Washing your hands
    d. Reporting and recording observations

Answers

1. c. Oral hygiene is cleansing the resident's mouth.

2. b. Immediately before performing oral hygiene the nurse assistant should assemble the equipment.

3. d. The nurse assistant can promote infection control by wearing gloves. Wearing gloves will prevent mouth secretions from touching the hands.

4. c. Oral hygiene for an unconscious resident requires the use of a tongue depressor and oral glycerine swabs.

5. a. Choking can be prevented by placing the unconscious resident's head to the side and using oral swabs when performing oral hygiene.

6. b. Lining the sink with a paper towel or water can prevent breakage if the dentures are accidentally dropped into the sink.

7. a. Dentures are rinsed in cold running water. Hot water may alter the shape of the dentures.

8. d. Abnormal conditions, such as cracks in the tongue, gum problems, sores, or a coated white tongue, are reported to the charge nurse.

9. a. Allowing the resident to assist, if able, will promote independence during the oral hygiene procedure.

10. d. The nurse assistant's responsibility after performing oral hygiene is handwashing, recording, and reporting any abnormalities immediately.

11. a. The nurse assistant should wash his or her hands prior to performing the bed bath procedure.

12. c. The nurse assistant should tactfully ask the visitors to leave and to return after the bed bath procedure is completed.

13. b. The nurse assistant should remove the spread, blanket, and top sheet prior to the bed bath procedure. The bath blanket and a large towel are used to provide privacy during the bed bath along with pulling the privacy curtain.

14. c. The correct water temperature during the bed bath is 115°F.

15. d. The face is washed first. Remember not to use soap unless the residents request you to do so.

16. a. The nurse assistant should change the wash basin water after washing the upper anterior body and whenever necessary.

17. b. The resident is given a back rub after washing the upper back and before washing the perineal area.

18. a. Abnormal observations during the bed bath are reported to the charge nurse in

long-term care facilities, and to the team leader in other health care settings.

19. c. Bedmaking is performed at the completion of the bed bath procedure.

20. d. The nurse assistant should secure the call signal.

21. d. The purpose of a tub bath is to cleanse the skin, promote relaxation, and increase circulation. The nurse assistant should also observe the skin for any abnormalities.

22. a. The nurse assistant should assemble all equipment prior to the tub bath.

23. b. The nurse assistant should disinfect the tub before and after a resident's use to promote infection control.

24. b. Electrical appliances should be removed to prevent contact with water.

25. b. The tub is filled half full to prevent overflow during the bath.

26. a. The correct water temperature is 105°F for a tub bath. The water should be tested with a bath thermometer.

27. c. A towel should be placed inside and outside of the tub to prevent slipping.

28. d. Never leave the resident unattended while he or she is in the bath tub.

29. c. Inflamed areas of skin should be reported to the charge nurse.

30. a. Documentation after completion of the bath should include completion, the resident's tolerance, and any abnormalities observed.

31. b. A back rub is applying lotion to the back and using long firm upward strokes and gentle downward strokes for approximately 1-1/2 to 3 minutes. The back rub increases circulation and promotes relaxation.

32. b. The nurse assistant should perform handwashing before beginning the back rub procedure.

33. d. Lotion, towel, and a wash basin with water at 115°F are assembled before the back rub procedure.

34. a. The positions most frequently used for the back rub procedure are the lateral, prone, left and right Sims'.

35. b. Before a back rub the nurse assistant should warm the lotion by placing the

lotion container in the basin of water at 115° for approximately five minutes.

36. d.   The lower back area is the area of the body where the nurse assistant should begin the back rub.

37. b.   Firm long upward strokes, gentle downward strokes, and circular motions on bony areas are rubbing methods for the back rub. Short gentle upward strokes are not used.

38. a.   A resident's standard back rub should consist of rubbing the back for 1-1/2 to 3 minutes.

39. c.   The resident should be placed in a side lying position after the back rub. However, the doctor may specifically order a prone position, but be careful to position the pillows correctly.

40. b.   A red open skin area is a stage 2 decubitus and should be reported to the charge nurse for treatment.

41. d.   Never use a straight razor to shave the resident. Always use a safety razor or electrical razor if permitted by your health care institution.

42. a.   Inspection of the skin is performed by the nurse assistant before attempting to shave a resident. If facial moles, or skin tags are noticed, be careful not to cut them during the shave.

43. c.   To soften the beard before the shave, apply warm water to the beard with a wash cloth.

44. b.   Shaving cream should be applied to the beard before attempting to shave the resident with a safety razor.

45. d.   The nurse assistant should hold the skin taut, shave in the direction of the hair growth, wear gloves and rinse the razor throughout the shaving procedure. Rinsing removes hair and shaving cream from the razor to facilitate smooth shaving during the procedure.

46. b.   The nurse assistant should direct the resident to keep the tongue in the hollow areas around the mouth, to assist in keeping the skin tight, and allow smooth shaving.

47. c.   Accidental nicks of the skin require the nurse assistant to report the incident to the charge nurse for follow-up care. Gentle pressure can be applied if bleeding persists.

48. b.   Before shaving the resident's beard, the nurse assistant should understand that shaving equipment may vary from resident to resident.

49. a.   To promote independence during the shaving procedure, allow the resident to assist, if able.

50. d.   After performing the shave, the nurse assistant should perform handwashing, place the call signal in reach, report and record, and leave the resident in a comfortable position.

51. b.   The nurse assistant should perform handwashing before beginning the nail care procedure.

52. d.   Nail care equipment assembled is a wash basin, soap, water at 105°F, orange stick, clippers, and emery board.

53. a.   The nails should be soaked and cleaned with soap and water at 105°F using the orange stick to remove dirt from under the nails.

54. c.   The hands should be rinsed and dried well before trimming the nails.

55. a.   The nurse assistant should trim the nails straight across, and smooth the rough edges with an emery board.

56. a.   The doctor should trim the diabetic resident's nails.

57. b.   An emery board is used to smooth the rough edges.

58. c.   Gentle massage from the finger tips towards the wrist helps the blood to circulate.

59. c.   The nurse assistant should secure the resident by raising the side rail, and placing the call signal within reach.

60. b.   The nurse assistant should report to the charge nurse if the nails are too difficult to trim.

61. c.   The nurse assistant should assemble the equipment before beginning the hair combing procedure.

62. b.   Equipment assembled for the hair combing procedure includes a towel, comb or brush, and a hand mirror.

63. d.   The nurse assistant should always check the identification armband before any procedure, for the safety of the resident.

64. b.   Promoting dignity is providing privacy, knocking on the door before entering,

calling the resident by his or her name, and allowing the resident's independence. Allow the resident to select his or her own hair styling.

65. c. The hair should be parted in sections to examine the scalp.

66. b. Hair lice should be reported immediately to the charge nurse.

67. b. Comb the resident's hair into the style the resident requests.

68. c. Suggest a braid to prevent tangling of the hair.

69. d. The nurse assistant should offer the resident a hand mirror for viewing after combing the hair.

70. b. After completing the hair combing procedure, the nurse assistant should make the resident comfortable, raise the side rails, open the curtain, place the call signal within the resident's reach, wash your hands, and report and record observations.

18

Elimination

Be sure to wear gloves.

1. Wash your hands before and after the procedure.
2. Greet the resident.
3. Check the armband.
4. Explain the procedure.
5. Assemble your equipment—urinal or bedpan, cover, tissue, and gloves.
6. Encourage the resident to assist if able.
7. Place the resident on the bedpan or position the urinal; allow the resident privacy.
8. Remove the bedpan or urinal; clean the resident if the resident is unable to do so.
9. Secure the resident.
10. Make the resident comfortable.
11. Place the call signal within reach.
12. Record and report observations to the charge nurse.

Position the resident to a side lying position, and center the bedpan.

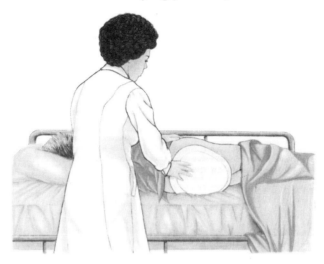

Roll the resident onto the bedpan.

QUESTIONS

DIRECTIONS: Each question contains four suggested responses. Select the one best response to each question.

ANSWERS: See answers at the end of the chapter.

1. Select the first action of the nurse assistant before offering the bedpan or urinal.
   a. Handwashing
   b. Explanation of the procedure
   c. Lowering the side rail
   d. Reporting to the charge nurse

2. Which one of the following sets of equipment is assembled before offering the bedpan or urinal?
   a. Wash basin and water at 105°F, toilet tissue, soap, bedpan or urinal cover, hand towel, and gloves
   b. Bedpan or urinal, wet wash cloth, toilet tissue, bedpan cover, and soap
   c. Bedpan or urinal and cover, toilet tissue, and gloves
   d. Wash basin with cold water, gloves, soap, bedpan, urinal, cover, and tissue

3. Select the appropriate method to assist a helpless resident on the bedpan.
   a. Lift the buttocks in an upward motion.
   b. Ask the resident to bend the knees and push up.

c. Elevate both legs upward and slide the bedpan under the buttocks.
   d. Turn the resident to the side and put the bedpan in place.

4. All of the following are appropriate actions after placing the resident on the bedpan EXCEPT:
   a. Raising the side rails
   b. Placing the toilet tissue and call signal within reach
   c. Leaving the room for privacy
   d. Staying at the resident's bedside

5. Which protective items are used when removing the bedpan?
   a. Gown, gloves, and masks are worn.
   b. Gloves and masks are worn.
   c. Gloves are worn.
   d. Gloves are not necessary.

6. Which one of the following observations of the bedpan contents is reported immediately?
   a. Moderate amount of soft brown stool
   b. Small amount of loose bloody stool
   c. Large amount of green loose stool
   d. Moderate amount of semi-formed stool

7. Select the appropriate method to clean a female resident after using the bedpan.
   a. Wipe from front to back.
   b. Wipe middle perineal or toward the front.
   c. Wipe from back to front.
   d. Any direction is appropriate.

8. Which one of the following statements is true regarding measuring output?
   a. Foods and liquids leaving the body are measured.
   b. Liquids entering and exiting the body are measured.
   c. Only liquids leaving the body are measured.
   d. Only liquids entering the body are measured.

9. Which one of the following observations is the nurse assistant likely to report when offering the incontinent resident a bedpan?
   a. Dry, clear intact skin
   b. Redden, irritated skin
   c. Clear urine
   d. Moderate amounts of urine

10. Select the appropriate response of the nurse assistant if the resident complains of frequency of urination.
    a. Report the information to the doctor.
    b. Offer cranberry juice.
    c. Encourage water.
    d. Report the information to the charge nurse.

RECORDING INTAKE AND OUTPUT

cc = cubic centimeter
ml = millimeter
oz = ounce
1 cc = 1 ml
$\frac{1}{4}$ teaspoon = 1 cc
1 teaspoon = 4 cc
30 cc = 1 oz
60 cc = 2 oz
90 cc = 3 oz
120 cc = 4 oz
150 cc = 5 oz
180 cc = 6 oz
210 cc = 7 oz
240 cc = 8 oz
270 cc = 9 oz
300 cc = 10 oz
500 cc = 1 pint
1000 cc = 1 quart
4000 cc = 1 gallon

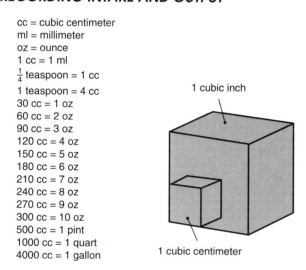

1 cubic inch

1 cubic centimeter

Liquids are recorded in cubic centimeters or cc's and milliliters or ml's.

MEASURING AND RECORDING OUTPUT

Empty the urine into the graduate.

REMEMBER

Wear gloves.

Place the graduate on a flat surface.

Obtain an accurate reading.

Be sure the urine is observed for abnormalities. For example: blood, mucus, cloudiness, or straw color. Report abnormalities to the charge nurse immediately.

1. Wash your hands before and after the procedure.

2. Greet the resident.

3. Check the armband.

4. Explain the procedure.

5. Assemble your equipment—gloves, graduate, intake and output form, and pen.

6. Provide privacy.

7. Total intake for the shift should be in the intake column.

8. Wear gloves and use the graduate to measure the output from the bedpan, urinal, or drainage bag.

9. Empty the urine into the graduate and place on a flat surface. Calculate according to the level of urine in the graduate. The graduate is calibrated to indicate numbers.

Use the numbers at the level of the urine to obtain an accurate urinary output value.

10. Record the amount on the intake and output form.

11. Open the curtain.

12. Secure the resident.

13. Place the call signal within reach.

14. Remove your gloves and wash your hands.

15. Report observations to the charge nurse.

QUESTIONS

DIRECTIONS: Each question contains four suggested responses. Select the one best response to each question.

ANSWERS: See answers at the end of the chapter.

11. Intake and output is best described as:
    a. Fluids leaving the resident's body
    b. Fluids entering the resident's body
    c. Fluids left in the resident's body
    d. A and B only

12. All of the following foods are calculated as intake EXCEPT:
    a. Milk
    b. Cheese
    c. Ice cream
    d. Juice

13. Fluid imbalance is best described as:
    a. Excessive amount of fluids retained in the body
    b. Excessive fluid released from the body
    c. Balance between food and liquids
    d. A or B

14. The volume measurement for liquids is abbreviated:
    a. ce
    b. ss
    c. cc
    d. ct

15. Calculate the resident's total intake of liquid with the following: 240 cc of coffee, 100 cc of milk, and 150 cc of juice.
    a. 460 cc
    b. 490 cc
    c. 590 cc
    d. 690 cc

16. Total intake is calculated:
    a. At the beginning of the shift
    b. During the shift
    c. At the end of each shift
    d. Throughout the shift

17. Which one of the following actions is appropriate if the nurse assistant observes a small amount of cloudy urine in the bedpan?
    a. Report the observation to the charge nurse.
    b. Encourage the resident to decrease milk.
    c. Encourage the resident to drink juice only.
    d. Encourage the resident to decrease water intake.

18. Fluid restriction is best described as:
    a. Limit the amounts of fluid per shift.
    b. Encourage 100 cc per hour per shift.
    c. Drink at least 1000 cc each shift.
    d. Have nothing by mouth.

19. Select the appropriate method to measure the urine voided into a bedpan.
    a. Estimate the amount.
    b. Pour the urine into the emesis basin.
    c. Pour the urine into a graduate placed on a flat surface.
    d. Pour the urine into a urinary drainage bag.

20. How many cubic centimeters are equivalent to 8 oz.?
    a. 140 cc
    b. 240 cc
    c. 340 cc
    d. 400 cc

CATHETER CARE

INDWELLING CATHETER

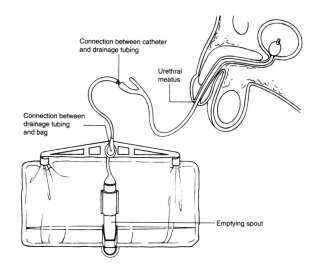

Connection between catheter and drainage tubing

Urethral meatus

Connection between drainage tubing and bag

Emptying spout

The bulb holds the catheter tube inside the bladder

1. Always keep the area around the catheter entry area clean.

2. Clean the catheter in a downward circular motion with a betadine swab.

3. Keep the tubing taped to the inner thigh to prevent a direct pull on the tube.

4. Never allow the bag to touch the floor.

5. Never raise the drainage bag higher than the bladder. This will prevent a return flow of urine to the bladder.

6. Always check the tubing for kinks.

7. Observe the urine for abnormalities.

8. Report leaking, lack of urine drainage, and abnormalities such as mucus, blood, and cloudiness to the charge nurse.

9. Be sure to wear gloves.

10. Don't use betadine if the resident is allergic to iodine.

11. Wash your hands before and after the procedure.

12. Greet the resident.

13. Check the armband.

14. Explain the procedure.

15. Assemble your equipment—gloves, betadine swabs, bath blanket, and a disposable bed protector.

16. Provide privacy.

17. Place the disposable bed protector under the buttock.

18. Swab the area around the catheter entry in a circular downward motion. Swab away from the catheter entry area to prevent microorganisms from entering the bladder.

19. Check the tubing for kinks.

20. Remove the disposable bed protector, remove the gloves, and wash your hands.

21. Make the resident comfortable.

22. Secure the resident.

23. Place the call signal within reach.

24. Open the curtain.

25. Wash your hands.

26. Record the procedure and report observations to the charge nurse.

QUESTIONS

DIRECTIONS: Each question contains suggested responses. Select the one best response to each question.

ANSWERS: See answers at the end of the chapter.

21. In which area of the excretory system is the indwelling catheter inflated to maintain placement?
    a. Kidney
    b. Ureter
    c. Bladder
    d. Urethra

22. Select the appropriate first response of the nurse assistant regarding a leaking indwelling catheter.
    a. Remove the catheter.
    b. Check the drainage bag.
    c. Check the tube for kinks.
    d. Report the leaking to the physician.

23. Which one of the following is the normal color of urine?
    a. Dark yellow and cloudy
    b. Straw color yellow
    c. Clear and yellow
    d. Orange and clear

24. When transferring a resident to the chair, the nurse assistant should always move the drainage bag:
    a. During the transfer
    b. Before the transfer
    c. After the transfer
    d. Does not matter; move at anytime

25. When should the nurse assistant empty the drainage bag?
    a. Beginning of the shift
    b. Middle of the shift
    c. After the shift
    d. After two shifts are completed

26. How should the nurse assistant measure the urine in the drainage bag?
    a. Estimate the amount.
    b. Drain the urine into a graduate.
    c. Follow the lines on the drainage bag.
    d. Drain the urine into the bedpan.

27. Which method of catheter care decreases the chance of microorganisms entering the bladder?
    a. Cleaning the catheter from the entry area downward
    b. Washing your hands after the catheter care
    c. Cleaning the catheter from the middle toward the entry area
    d. Cleaning the catheter from the drainage tubing upward

28. Which method should the nurse assistant follow to provide catheter care?
    a. Use betadine swabs.
    b. Cleanse around the catheter entry area.
    c. Begin at the catheter entry area and clean downward.
    d. All of the above.

29. Select the appropriate method to prevent direct contact with the drainage around the catheter tube.
    a. Hold the catheter with a tissue.
    b. Wear gloves.
    c. Wash your hands during the procedure.
    d. Wash the perineal area.

30. Which one of the following actions would prevent the urine in the drainage bag from returning to the bladder?
    a. Holding the bag higher than the bladder
    b. Attaching the catheter tube to the inside of the thigh
    c. Clapping the catheter tube while in bed
    d. Holding the bag below the level of the bladder

Answers

1. a. The nurse assistant should perform hand-washing before offering the bedpan or urinal.

2. a. The following equipment is assembled before offering the bedpan or urinal: wash basin and water at 105°F, soap, toilet tissue, bedpan or urinal, gloves, and a hand towel.

3. d. To assist a helpless resident on the bedpan, turn the resident to the side, place the bedpan next to buttock, and roll the resident over with the bedpan centered for comfort.

4. d. The nurse assistant should place the toilet tissue and call signal in reach, raise the side rail, and leave the room to allow the resident privacy.

5. c. Gloves should be worn when removing the bedpan or urinal.

6. b. Small amounts of loose bloody stool should be reported to the charge nurse immediately.

7. a. The female resident is wiped from front to back to prevent stool from being introduced into the urethra. Proper wiping techniques can help prevent bladder infections.

8. c. Output measuring includes all liquids leaving the body.

9. b. The incontinent resident is likely to have reddened irritated skin because of inability to control urinary output.

10. d. The nurse assistant should report the complaint to the charge nurse. The charge nurse will notify the physician for new orders.

11. d. Fluids going into the body and fluids leaving the body are classified as intake and output.

12. b. Cheese is a solid food and is not calculated as intake.

13. d. Fluid imbalance is an excessive amount of fluids retained or excessive amounts of fluid released, causing the body to be in fluid imbalance.

14. c. The nurse assistant should record liquid measurements in cubic centimeters, which is abbreviated cc, and in milliliters, abbreviated ml.

15. b. The total intake is 490 cc.

16. c. The nurse assistant should total the resident's intake at the end of the shift.

17. a. Report the observation to the charge nurse.

18. a. A limited amount of fluid each shift is fluid restriction.

19. c. The nurse assistant should pour the urine into a graduate placed on a flat surface to obtain an accurate measurement.

20. b. 8 oz. is equivalent to 240 cc.

21. c. The indwelling catheter is inflated in the bladder to maintain placement.

22. c. The nurse assistant should check the tubing for kinks.

23. c. The normal color of urine is clear and yellow.

24. b. The drainage bag is moved first to prevent pulling the indwelling catheter from the bladder.

25. c. The drainage bag should be emptied at the end of the shift, and whenever necessary.

26. b. The nurse assistant should drain the urine from the drainage bag into a graduate cylinder for accurate measuring.

27. a. Cleaning the catheter from the entry area downward decreases the chance of microorganisms entering the bladder via the catheter.

28. d. To remove organisms on the catheter tube, the nurse assistant should use an antiseptic solution, preferably betadine swabs, and clean in a downward motion away from the catheter entry area.

29. b. Gloves will prevent direct contact with drainage around the catheter tube.

30. d. The drainage bag should always be held below the level of the bladder. Preventing a return flow of urine into the bladder decreases the chance of a bladder infection.

19

Measuring and Recording Vital Signs

METHODS OF MEASURING BODY TEMPERATURE

1. Oral
2. Electronic
3. Rectal
4. Axillary

TAKING AN ORAL TEMPERATURE

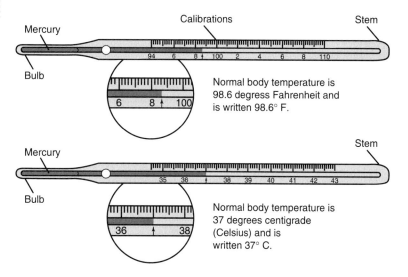

Normal body temperature is 98.6 degress Fahrenheit and is written 98.6° F.

Normal body temperature is 37 degrees centigrade (Celsius) and is written 37° C.

Measuring the temperature with an oral thermometer

MEASURING THE ORAL TEMPERATURE

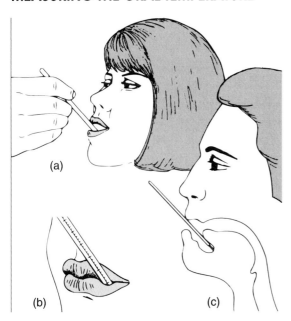

(a)

(b)   (c)

Insert the thermometer under the tongue

1. Wash your hands before and after the procedure.

2. Greet the resident.

3. Check the armband.

4. Explain the procedure.

5. Assemble your equipment—oral thermometer, thermometer cover (sheath), tissue, pad, and pencil.

6. Provide privacy.

7. Provide safety.

8. Perform the procedure—shake down the mercury, place the cover over the thermometer, insert the thermometer to the side of the mouth under the tongue for 8 minutes. Follow the policy and procedures of your health care institution.

9. Remove the thermometer, discard the sheath, wipe the thermometer with the tissue and record the results.

10. Secure the resident.

11. Place the call signal within reach.

12. Report observations to the charge nurse.

QUESTIONS

DIRECTIONS: Each question contains four suggested responses. Select the one best response to each question.

ANSWERS: See answers at the end of the chapter.

1. Which one of the following is the first action of the nurse assistant before measuring the resident's body heat?
   a. Wash hands.
   b. Assemble the equipment.
   c. Shake the thermometer below 95°F.
   d. Explain the procedure.

2. Select the basic piece of equipment required to measure the resident's body heat.
   a. Stethoscope
   b. Watch
   c. Thermometer
   d. Sphygmomanometer

3. While performing the oral temperature procedure, handwashing is performed immediately before which nursing task?
   a. Before assembling equipment
   b. Before identifying the resident
   c. Before the explanation of the procedure
   d. Before greeting the resident

4. Select the appropriate action of the nurse assistant before taking a resident's temperature.
   a. Check the thermometer for cracks.
   b. Clean the thermometer with hot, soapy water.
   c. Make sure the mercury is above 96°F.
   d. Wait 5 minutes after eating or drinking.

5. A thermometer sheath is best described as:
   a. A brown plastic cover placed over the thermometer before use.
   b. A clear plastic cover is placed over thermometer before use.

c. Equipment used for thermometer storage.
d. A device used to cleanse a thermometer.

6. Select the appropriate length of time to leave the thermometer in place for the oral temperature procedure.
   a. 1 to 2 minutes
   b. 3 to 8 minutes
   c. 9 to 10 minutes
   d. 5 to 6 minutes

7. In which direction should the nurse assistant wipe the thermometer after removing it from the resident's mouth?
   a. Wipe from the bulb upward.
   b. Begin at the middle of the thermometer and wipe upward.
   c. Wipe the stem from top to bottom.
   d. Wipe the bulb only.

8. A thermometer reading of 37° centigrade is equivalent to which of the following?
   a. 98.6°F
   b. 97°F

c. 99°F
d. 100°F

9. All of the following are normal oral temperature readings EXCEPT:
   a. 96.6°F
   b. 97.6°F
   c. 98.6°F
   d. 99°F

10. Which one of the following temperatures should be reported after completing the oral temperature procedure?
    a. 97.6°F
    b. 98.6°F
    c. 99.6°F
    d. 100.6°F

TAKING AN ORAL TEMPERATURE USING AN ELECTRONIC THERMOMETER

1. Wash your hands before and after the procedure.

2. Greet the resident.

3. Check the armband.

4. Explain the procedure.

5. Assemble your equipment—electronic thermometer, plastic probe cover, gloves, TPR form, and pen.

6. Provide privacy.

7. Provide safety.

8. Place the plastic probe cover over the electronic thermometer, insert the probe under the tongue and wait 15 seconds or until the electronic beeper sounds. Record the results.

9. Discard the plastic probe cover.

10. Place the resident in a comfortable position.

11. Open the privacy curtain.

12. Raise the side rails.

13. Remove your gloves and wash your hands.

14. Report the observations to the charge nurse.

DIRECTIONS: Each question contains four suggested responses. Select the one best response to each question.
ANSWERS: See answers at the end of the chapter.

11. All of the following equipment is assembled to take an oral electronic temperature EXCEPT:
    a. Disposable plastic probe cover
    b. Electronic thermometer
    c. Oral blue attachment
    d. Glass thermometer

12. Handwashing is performed how often during the electronic temperature procedure?
    a. Once
    b. Twice
    c. Three times
    d. Not at all

13. Identification of the resident is performed:
    a. After handwashing
    b. Before handwashing
    c. After providing privacy
    d. Before the equipment is assembled

14. Select the appropriate action of the nurse assistant to relieve the resident's apprehension before a procedure.
    a. Wash hands
    b. Pull the privacy curtain.
    c. Explain the procedure.
    d. Raise the side rail.

15. Observation of the electronic thermometer for proper functioning is performed by which staff member?
    a. Janitor
    b. Charge nurse
    c. Ward clerk
    d. Nurse assistant

16. Select the appropriate position in which to place the covered probe of the electronic thermometer in the resident's mouth.
    a. Roof of the mouth
    b. Top of the tongue
    c. Directly under the tongue
    d. Between the teeth and jaw

17. Which one of the following sounds would indicate that the electronic temperature is completed?
    a. Beeping
    b. Horn sound
    c. Computer voice
    d. Absence of sound

18. All of the following are normal oral temperature readings EXCEPT:
    a. 97.6°F
    b. 96.8°F
    c. 98.6°F
    d. 98.2°F

19. All of the following are performed after taking the oral electronic temperature EXCEPT:
    a. Handwashing
    b. Returning the electronic thermometer to the storage area
    c. Reporting and recording the temperature
    d. Storing the electronic thermometer with the probe cover in place

20. Which one of the following oral temperature readings should be reported to the charge nurse?
    a. 99°F
    b. 98.6°F
    c. 100°F
    d. 97.8°F

MEASURING THE RECTAL TEMPERATURE

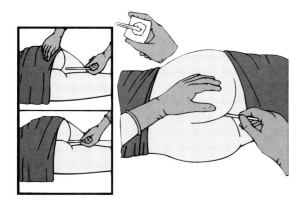

Place the resident in a side lying position with only the buttocks exposed

- Expose only the buttocks.
- Lubricate before insertion of the thermometer.

1. Wash your hands before and after the procedure.

2. Greet the resident.

3. Check the armband.

4. Explain the procedure.

5. Assemble your equipment—gloves, rectal thermometer (red tip, sheath, lubricating jel, tissue, TPR form, and pen.

6. Provide privacy.

7. Put on the gloves.

8. Position the resident to a side lying position. Check the thermometer for defects. Be sure to shake down the mercury, cover the thermometer, and lubricate the bulb.

9. Expose only the buttocks. Hold the buttocks open. Insert thermometer 1 inch into the rectum; hold in place for 3 minutes.

10. Remove the thermometer; wipe the stem downward with the tissue. Discard the tissue and sheath.

11. Place the resident in a comfortable position.

12. Secure the resident. Open the curtain, and place the call signal within reach.

13. Remove your gloves and wash your hands.

14. Record and report the temperature to the charge nurse.

QUESTIONS

DIRECTIONS: Each question contains four suggested responses. Select the one best response to each question.

ANSWERS: See answers at the end of the chapter.

21. Which one of the following tasks should the nurse assistant perform *first* before taking a rectal temperature?
    a. Explain the procedure.
    b. Wash hands
    c. Assemble the equipment.
    d. Pull the curtain.

22. Select the equipment used for the rectal temperature and not used for the oral temperature.
    a. Gloves
    b. Lubricating jelly
    c. Tissue
    d. Temperature board

23. A red-tip thermometer is used for which temperature procedure?
    a. Oral
    b. Axillary
    c. Femoral
    d. Rectal

24. Inspection of the thermometer for cracks or chips is performed by which staff member?
    a. Nurse assistant
    b. Coworker
    c. Janitor
    d. Central supply

25. Lubricating jelly is used during a rectal temperature for which purpose?
    a. To hold the thermometer in place
    b. To speed up the process
    c. To allow easy insertion
    d. To receive an accurate reading

26. In which position should the nurse assistant place the resident for the rectal temperature procedure?
    a. Sims'
    b. Supine
    c. Fowler's
    d. Dangling

27. Select the appropriate depth to insert the rectal thermometer.
    a. 1/2 inch
    b. 1 inch
    c. 2 inches
    d. 3 inches

28. Which abbreviation should the nurse assistant place next to the temperature to indicate a rectal temperature was taken?
    a. R
    b. RT
    c. Rec
    d. RE

29. All of the following are performed during a rectal temperature EXCEPT:
    a. Lubricating the bulb
    b. Wearing gloves
    c. Holding the thermometer in place 3 minutes
    d. Allowing the resident privacy after inserting the thermometer

30. Which one of the following rectal temperatures should be reported?
    a. 98.6°F
    b. 99°F
    c. 101°F
    d. 100°F

....

MEASURING THE AXILLARY TEMPERATURE

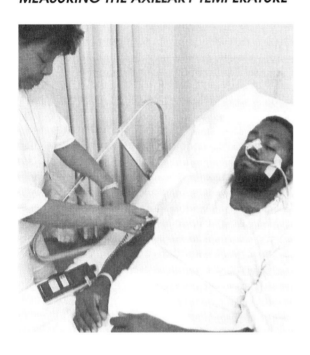

Dry the armpit thoroughly before placing the thermometer in place.

1. Wash your hands before and after the procedure.

2. Greet the resident.

3. Check the armband.

4. Explain the procedure.

5. Assemble your equipment—gloves, tissues, thermometer, sheath, TPR form, and pen.

6. Provide privacy.

7. Put on gloves.

8. Dry the armpit thoroughly.

9. Shake the mercury below 95°F, cover the thermometer with a sheath.

10. Place the thermometer in the axillary area for 10 minutes.

11. Wipe clean with tissue. Record the results.

12. Place the resident in a comfortable position.

13. Secure the resident.

14. Open the curtain, and place the call signal within reach.

15. Remove your gloves and wash your hands.

16. Record and report observations to the charge nurse.

DIRECTIONS: Each question contains four suggested responses. Select the one best response to each question.

ANSWERS: See answers at the end of the chapter.

31. Select the first action of the nurse assistant before measuring an axillary temperature.
    a. Assembling the equipment
    b. Handwashing
    c. Pulling the curtain
    d. Explaining the procedure

32. All of the following is equipment used to measure the axillary temperature EXCEPT:
    a. Thermometer
    b. Lubricant
    c. Towel
    d. Thermometer sheath

33. Handwashing is performed how often during the axillary temperature procedure?
    a. Not at all
    b. Once
    c. Twice
    d. Three times

34. Select the appropriate action of the nurse assistant if the resident refuses the axillary temperature procedure.
    a. Verbally force the resident
    b. Report the resident to a family member
    c. Physically force the resident
    d. Report the incident to the charge nurse

35. What should the nurse assistant understand about axillary temperatures?
    a. Axillary temperature is the most accurate.
    b. Axillary temperature is the least accurate.
    c. Axillary temperature is the most convenient.
    d. Axillary temperature requires less time.

36. Select the appropriate action of the nurse assistant before taking an axillary temperature.
    a. Shave the armpit.
    b. Wash the armpit.
    c. Dry the armpit.
    d. Apply alcohol to the armpit.

37. Axillary temperatures require the nurse assistant to leave the thermometer in place for how long?
    a. 5 minutes
    b. 10 minutes
    c. 15 minutes
    d. 20 minutes

38. Which staff member is required to cleanse the thermometer after use?
    a. Central supply technician
    b. Ward clerk
    c. Janitor
    d. Nurse assistant

39. Which one of the following axillary temperatures should the nurse assistant report to the charge nurse.
    a. 96.6°F
    b. 97.6°F
    c. 98.6°F
    d. 99.6°F

40. All of the following are performed after completion of the axillary temperature procedure EXCEPT:
    a. Handwashing
    b. Lowering the side rail
    c. Placing the call signal in reach
    d. Reporting and recording

MEASURING THE PULSE PROCEDURE

MEASURING THE RADIAL PULSE

The radial artery is located on the thumb side of the wrist. Never use the thumb to find the artery because the thumb has a pulse of its own.

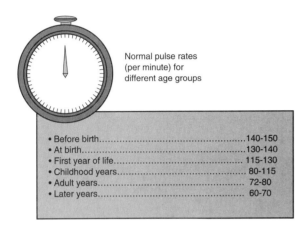

Normal pulse rates (per minute) for different age groups

• Before birth	140-150
• At birth	130-140
• First year of life	115-130
• Childhood years	80-115
• Adult years	72-80
• Later years	60-70

Various pulse ranges

1. Wash your hands before and after the procedure.

2. Greet the resident.

3. Check the armband.

4. Explain the procedure.

5. Assemble your equipment—TPR form, pen, and watch with a second hand.

6. Provide privacy.

7. Locate the radial artery on the thumb side of wrist and use the first three fingers, not the thumb. Press gently to find the pulse.

8. Count the pulse for 1 minute.

9. Record the pulse.

10. Reposition the resident for comfort.

11. Secure the resident.

12. Place the call signal within reach.

13. Report observations to the charge nurse.

QUESTIONS

DIRECTIONS: Each question contains four suggested responses. Select the one best response to each question.

ANSWERS: See answers at the end of the chapter.

41. Select the first action of the nurse assistant before taking the resident's pulse.
    a. Explain the procedure
    b. Wash hands.
    c. Provide privacy
    d. Assemble the equipment

42. All of the following equipment is assembled for the radial pulse procedure EXCEPT:
    a. Stethoscope
    b. Vital sign clipboard
    c. Watch with a second hand
    d. Pen or pencil

43. How often should the nurse assistant perform handwashing during the pulse-taking procedure?
    a. Before the procedure

    b. Before and after the procedure
    c. After the procedure
    d. After locating the radial artery

44. Which one of the following principles would *encourage* the resident's cooperation during the pulse-taking procedure?
    a. Infection control
    b. Independence
    c. Communication
    d. Safety

45. Which one of the following areas should the nurse assistant feel for the radial pulse?
    a. Thumb side of the inner wrist
    b. Baby finger side of the wrist
    c. Middle wrist area
    d. Left chest area

46. On which body area should the nurse assistant place the stethoscope to take an apical pulse?
    a. Left chest area

b. Right chest area

c. Wrist area

d. Right upper back area

47. Select the appropriate method used by the nurse assistant to perform the radial pulse procedure.

    a. Place the thumb over the radial artery.

    b. Place the first three fingers over the radial artery.

    c. Place the index finger only over the radial artery.

    d. Place the first two fingers over the radial artery.

48. Select the appropriate method to count an irregular pulse rate.

    a. Count for 15 seconds and multiply by 4.

    b. Count for 30 seconds and multiply by 2.

    c. Count for 1 full minute.

    d. Count for 10 seconds and divide by 2.

49. Which one of the following pulse rates should the nurse assistant report to the charge nurse?

    a. Adult pulse rate below 60

    b. Adult pulse rate of 72 to 80

    c. Newborn pulse rate of 132

    d. Toddler pulse rate of 100

50. All of the following are performed after completion of the pulse-taking procedure EXCEPT:

    a. Reporting and recording observations

    b. Handwashing

    c. Placing the call signal in reach

    d. Explain the procedure

MEASURING THE RESPIRATION PROCEDURE

MEASURING THE RESPIRATION

Take the respiration without the resident being aware to prevent alteration of breathing.

• One inhale and one exhale is one complete respiration.

1. Wash your hands before and after the procedure.

2. Greet the resident.

3. Check the armband.

4. Explain the procedure.

5. Assemble your equipment—watch with a second hand, TPR form, and pen.

6. Provide privacy.

7. Pretend to take the pulse; count one inhale and one exhale as one respiration.

8. Count for 1 minute.

9. Record the respiration.

10. Reposition the resident for comfort.

11. Secure the resident.

12. Place the call signal within reach.

13. Report observations to the charge nurse.

DIRECTIONS: Each question contains four suggested responses. Select the one best response to each question.

ANSWERS: See answers at the end of the chapter.

51. Select the first action of the nurse assistant before taking the resident's respiration.
    a. Explain the procedure.
    b. Wash hands
    c. Assemble your equipment.
    d. Ask the charge nurse's permission.

52. All of the following equipment is used to measure the resident's respiration EXCEPT:
    a. Watch with a second hand
    b. Pen or pencil
    c. Vital sign clipboard
    d. Stethoscope

53. Select the action of the nurse assistant immediately before taking the resident's respiration.
    a. Handwashing.
    b. Identifying the resident.
    c. Pulling the curtain.
    d. Politely asking visitors to leave (if this is your hospital's policy).

54. All of the following are actions of the nurse assistant while measuring the respiration EXCEPT:
    a. Holding the wrist while taking the pulse
    b. Making sure the resident is aware that his or her respiration is being taken
    c. Never telling the resident that his or her respiration is being taken
    d. Beginning the pulse procedure before taking the respiration

55. Select the appropriate method to take a child's temperature, pulse, and respiration.
    a. Take the temperature first.
    b. Take the respiration first.
    c. Take the respiration and pulse first.
    d. Take the pulse and temperature first.

56. Which one of the following methods are used to take an accurate respiration?
    a. Count one chest rise as one respiration.
    b. Count two chest rises as one respiration.
    c. Count each chest rise as two respirations.
    d. Count one rise and fall of the chest as one respiration.

57. All of the following are normal respiratory rates EXCEPT:
    a. 24
    b. 20
    c. 18
    d. 16

58. Select the appropriate method to count an irregular respiratory rate.
    a. Count for 15 seconds, multiply by 4.
    b. Count for 30 seconds, multiply by 2.
    c. Count for 60 seconds, multiply by 0.
    d. Count for 2 full minutes.

59. All of the following terms refer to respiratory difficulty EXCEPT:
    a. Dyspnea
    b. Pneumonia
    c. Asthma
    d. Edema

60. To which team member should the nurse assistant report any abnormal respiratory observations?
    a. Charge nurse
    b. Director of nurses
    c. Supervisor
    d. Coworker/nurse assistant

MEASURING THE BLOOD PRESSURE PROCEDURE

Measuring the Blood Pressure

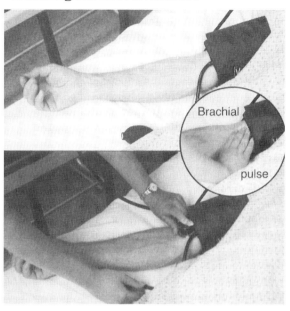

Identify brachial artery before taking the blood pressure.

Place the stethoscope over the brachial artery located at the inner aspect of the elbow

1. Wash your hands before and after the procedure.
2. Greet the resident.
3. Check the armband.
4. Explain the procedure.
5. Assemble your equipment: stethoscope, sphygmomanometer (blood pressure cuff), alcohol pad, TPR form, and pen.
6. Provide privacy.
7. Identify the brachial artery. Place the blood pressure cuff above the elbow, place the stethoscope over the artery, and take the blood pressure.
8. Record the results.
9. Reposition the resident for comfort.
10. Secure the resident.
11. Place the call signal within reach.
12. Report observations to the charge nurse.

QUESTIONS

DIRECTIONS: Each question contains four suggested responses. Select the one best response to each question.

ANSWERS: See answers at the end of the chapter.

61. Select the first action of the nurse assistant before measuring the resident's blood pressure.
    a. Explain the procedure.
    b. Assemble your equipment.
    c. Pull the curtain.
    d. Lower the side rail.

62. All of the following equipment is assembled for the blood pressure procedure EXCEPT:
    a. Sphygmomanometer
    b. Stethoscope and antiseptic pad
    c. Vital sign clipboard and pen
    d. Watch with a second hand

63. How often is handwashing performed during the blood pressure procedure?
    a. Not at all
    b. Once
    c. Twice
    d. Three times

64. Select the appropriate action of the nurse assistant to cleanse the earplugs of the stethoscope.
    a. Antiseptic pad
    b. Soap and water
    c. Hydrogen peroxide
    d. Betadine

65. Select the appropriate artery on which to place the stethoscope to measure the resident's blood pressure.
    a. Radial
    b. Carotid
    c. Brachial
    d. Temporal

66. Which one of the following statements should the nurse assistant understand regarding placement of the blood pressure cuff?
    a. Place the cuff snugly below the elbow.

b. Place the cuff 2 inches below the shoulder.

c. Place the cuff snugly above the elbow.

d. Place the cuff snugly around the wrist.

67. Select the blood pressure reading that indicates an elevated systolic pressure.
    a. 120/90
    b. 160/90
    c. 140/100
    d. 130/100

68. All of the following blood pressures are abnormal and should be reported to the charge nurse EXCEPT:
    a. 140/80
    b. 100/50

c. 160/100

d. 90/40

69. Select the normal adult range for a blood pressure reading.
    a. 70 /30 to 130/90
    b. 90/60 to 140/90
    c. 110/140 to 70/90
    d. 80/140 to 60/90

70. All of the following are performed after completion of the blood pressure procedure EXCEPT:
    a. Handwashing
    b. Placing the call signal within reach
    c. Cleansing the stethoscope with hot water
    d. Reporting and record information

Answers

1. a. Handwashing is performed before beginning the oral temperature procedures.

2. c. The equipment assembled is a thermometer, sheath or cover, gloves, pen, and vital sign clipboard.

3. d. Handwashing is performed immediately before greeting the resident.

4. a. Before taking a resident's temperature, the nurse assistant should check the thermometer for cracks.

5. b. A thermometer sheath is a clear plastic cover placed over the thermometer before use.

6. b. The thermometer is left in place 3 to 8 minutes. Follow your institution's policies and procedures.

7. c. Wipe the thermometer stem from the top to the bottom to cleanse it.

8. a. 37° centigrade is equivalent to 98.6° Fahrenheit.

9. a. The normal adult oral temperature range is 97.6°F to 99.6°F. An oral temperature of 96.6°F should be reported as this reading is not in the normal adult range.

10. d. The temperature reading of 100.6°F would be reported to the charge nurse. The normal oral adult range is 97.6°F to 99.6°F.

11. d. A glass thermometer is not necessary to take an electronic temperature. The electronic thermometer will give an accurate temperature in approximately 15 seconds.

12. b. The nurse assistant should wash hands before and after the procedure.

13. a. The resident's identification armband is checked after handwashing.

14. c. An explanation of the procedure will decrease the resident's apprehension about the procedure.

15. d. The nurse assistant should check all equipment for proper functioning before using.

16. c. The covered electronic probe should be placed directly under the tongue, slightly to the side of the mouth.

17. a. The electronic thermometer will beep in approximately 15 seconds to signal completion of the oral temperature.

18. b. The normal oral temperature can range from 97°F to 99°F.

19. d. After the completion of electronic temperature procedure the nurse assistant should remove the used probe and discard it in the trash, wash hands, and report and record any observations.

20. c. The nurse assistant should report an oral temperature reading of 100°.

21. b. The nurse assistant should perform handwashing before beginning the procedure.

22. b. Lubricating jelly is used in the rectal temperature procedure to allow easy insertion of the rectal thermometer.

23. d. The nurse assistant should use a rectal thermometer, which is identified with a red tip, for the rectal temperature procedure.

24. a. The nurse assistant should inspect the thermometer for cracks or chips before use.

25. c. Lubricating jelly is applied to the bulb end of the rectal thermometer to allow easy insertion into the rectum.

26. a. The right or left Sims' position is a side lying position and is the desirable position for the rectal temperature procedure.

27. b. The rectal thermometer should be inserted at least 1 inch and held in place approximately 3 minutes to obtain an accurate reading.

28. a. The nurse assistant should place R next to the rectal temperature to indicate it was taken rectally.

29. d. The nurse assistant should lubricate the bulb, wear gloves, and hold the thermometer in place. Never leave the resident unattended during the rectal temperature procedure.

30. c. A rectal temperature of 101°F or above should be reported to the charge nurse.

31. b. The nurse assistant should perform handwashing before any procedure.

32. b. Lubrication is not necessary for an axillary temperature. The nurse assistant should assemble thermometer, towel, and thermometer sheath to measure an axillary temperature.

33. c. Handwashing is performed before and after each procedure

34. d. The nurse assistant should try to encourage the resident. If this is not effective, report the incident to the charge nurse.

35. b. The nurse assistant should understand that the axillary temperature is the least accurate.

36. c. The armpit should be dried before the axillary temperature is measured.

37. b. The nurse assistant should allow the thermometer to stay in place for 10 minutes.

38. d. Thermometers are cleansed after each use by the nurse assistant.

39. d. Axillary temperatures above 99.6°F should be reported to the charge nurse.

40. b. The nurse assistant should raise the side rail to ensure the resident's safety.

41. b. Before beginning the pulse procedure the nurse assistant should perform the handwashing procedure.

42. a. Equipment assembled for the radial pulse procedure is a watch with a second hand, vital sign clipboard, and a pen or pencil.

43. b. Handwashing is performed before and after the pulse-taking procedure.

44. c. The principle of communication, which is an explanation of the pulse-taking procedure, will encourage the resident's cooperation.

45. a. The nurse assistant should feel for the radial pulse on the thumb side of the inner wrist area.

46. a. The stethoscope is placed over the apex of the heart, which is located in the left chest cavity.

47. b. The nurse assistant should place the first three fingers over the radial artery to take the resident's radial pulse.

48. c. The accurate method to count an irregular pulse is to count the pulse for a full minute or 60 seconds.

49. a. An adult pulse rate below 60 is reported to the charge nurse.

50. d. An explanation of the procedure is performed before the pulse-taking procedure. After completion of the procedure the nurse assistant should make the resident comfortable, place the call signal within reach, raise the side rail, open the curtain, wash hands, and report and record observations.

51. b. The nurse assistant should perform handwashing before taking the resident's respiration.

52. d. Equipment used to take the resident's respiration is a watch with a second hand, pen or pencil, and vital sign clipboard. The stethoscope is not used to take the respiration.

53. c. The nurse assistant should pull the curtain for the resident's privacy immediately before taking the resident's respiration.

54. b. Never let the resident know you are taking his or her respiration, because the res-

ident could possibly alter his or her breathing pattern.

55. c. The appropriate method to take a child's vital signs is to take the respiration, pulse, and then the temperature.

56. d. Count one rise and one fall of the resident's chest as one respiration.

57. a. A respiratory rate of 24 is not within the normal adult range of 16 to 20.

58. c. Count the irregular respiration for 1 full minute or 60 seconds.

59. d. Edema is not a term referring to respiratory difficulty. Edema is swelling commonly seen in the face, hands, and lower extremities.

60. a. The nurse assistant should report any abnormal respiratory observations to the charge nurse.

61. a. The nurse assistant should explain the procedure before measuring the blood pressure.

62. d. Equipment assembled for the blood pressure procedure is sphygmomanometer, stethoscope, antiseptic pad, pen or pencil, and the vital sign clipboard. A watch with a second hand is not needed to measure the resident's blood pressure.

63. c. Handwashing is performed before and after the blood pressure procedure.

64. a. To cleanse the earplugs of the stethoscope, the nurse assistant should use an antiseptic pad or solution.

65. c. The appropriate artery on which to place the diaphragm of the stethoscope is the brachial artery.

66. c. The sphygmomanometer or blood pressure cuff should be placed snugly above the elbow.

67. b. The blood pressure reading of 160/90 indicates an elevated systolic reading. The number 160 is an elevated systolic blood pressure reading.

68. a. A blood pressure reading of 140/80 is normal. Abnormal vital signs should be reported immediately to the charge nurse.

69. b. The normal adult range for blood pressures can be as low as 90/60 and high as 140/90.

70. c. The nurse assistant should make the resident comfortable, open the curtain, raise the side rail, place the call signal within reach, wash your hands, report and record information, and cleanse the earplugs of the stethoscope with an antiseptic solution.

20

First Aid for an Obstructed Airway
(Conscious Resident)

FIRST AID FOR AN OBSTRUCTED AIRWAY
(Conscious Resident)

Distress signal of choking

Place the thumb side of fist next to the abdomen 2" above the navel.

Give rapid inward and upward abdominal thrusts until the object is dislodged.

If the resident is pregnant, or obese, place your arms around the chest area to dislodge the obstruction.

1. Ask the resident if he or she can speak.

2. If there is no response, assist the resident to a standing position.

3. Position yourself behind the resident.

4. Place the thumb side of your fist next to the abdomen, 2 inches above the navel.

5. Give rapid inward and upward abdominal thrusts until object is dislodged.

6. Recheck the resident's airway.

7. Place the resident in an upright sitting position.

8. Secure the resident.

9. Place the call signal within reach.

10. Wash your hands.

11. Record and report observations to the charge nurse.

QUESTIONS

DIRECTIONS: Each question contains four suggested responses. Select the one best response to each question.

ANSWERS: See answers at the end of the questions.

1. Select the first action of the nurse assistant before assisting a resident with an obstructed airway.
   a. Deliver four quick blows to the back.
   b. Ask the resident if he or she can speak.
   c. Perform the finger sweep.
   d. Go and inform the charge nurse.

2. Which one of the following observations would tell the nurse assistant that the resident's airway is completely obstructed?
   a. The resident verbally tells the nurse assistant.
   b. A coworker tells the nurse assistant.
   c. The resident is holding his or her neck and not making a sound.
   d. The resident is making a clear coughing sound and tearing.

3. All of the following are performed by the nursing assistant before deciding that the resident's airway is obstructed EXCEPT:
   a. Turning on the resident's call signal.
   b. Asking the resident if he or she can speak.
   c. Looking, listening, and feeling for the signs of complete obstruction.
   d. Leaving the resident unattended.

4. Select the appropriate action of the nurse assistant after establishing complete airway obstruction.
   a. Give four back blows.
   b. Perform CPR.
   c. Perform the Heimlich maneuver.
   d. Turn on the resident's call signal.

5. Which one of the following positions should the nurse assistant understand to be an effective position to assist with an obstructed airway?
   a. Standing behind the resident
   b. Standing toward the front, facing the resident
   c. Standing on the left side of the resident
   d. Standing to the right side of the resident

6. All of the following methods are performed during the Heimlich Maneuver EXCEPT:
   a. Positioning yourself behind the resident
   b. Placing your arms around the resident's midsection
   c. Making a fist and placing the thumb side against the midline
   d. Placing your arms around the resident's chest

7. How often should the nurse assistant perform abdominal thrusts?
   a. One to two
   b. Three to four
   c. Five times

d. Until object is dislodged

8. Abdominal thrusts are best described as:
   a. Applying inward, upward rapid pressure to the midsection
   b. Applying pressure to the chest cavity
   c. Applying rapid pressure to lower abdomen
   d. Applying pressure to the lower sternum

9. Select the appropriate action of the nurse assistant after the resident's obstruction is dislodged.
   a. Allow the resident to continue to eat.
   b. Give the resident a drink of water.
   c. Place the resident in a high Fowler position.
   d. Place the resident in a supine position.

10. All of the following nursing tasks are performed after clearing the resident's obstructed airway EXCEPT:
    a. Taking the vital signs and washing your hands
    b. Encouraging the resident to sit upright
    c. Reporting to the charge nurse
    d. Offering fluids to the resident.

Answers

1. b. The nurse assistant should ask the resident if he or she can speak.

2. c. A resident holding his or her neck and unable to make a sound is a good indication that the airway is completely obstructed.

3. d. The nurse assistant should never leave the resident unattended when he or she suspects an airway obstruction.

4. c. The Heimlich maneuver is performed after establishing that the resident's airway is completely obstructed. If the resident can make sounds, allow the resident to clear his or her own airway if able.

5. a. The nurse assistant should be positioned behind the resident to place arms around the resident's midline.

6. d. The nurse assistant should place his or her arms around the resident's midline, make a fist and place the thumb side of the first against the midline of the resident's abdomen, slightly above the navel.

7. d. Abdominal thrusts should be performed until object is dislodged.

8. a. Abdominal thrusts are described as applying rapid inward and upward pressure to the midline, between the navel and the rib cage.

9. c. After dislodging the obstruction, the nurse assistant should place the resident in a high Fowler position to facilitate breathing.

10. d. The nurse assistant should make the resident comfortable, place him or her in a high Fowler position, wash hands, and report to the charge nurse. Never offer the resident fluids, this could cause further problems.

21

Assisting the Resident to Eat

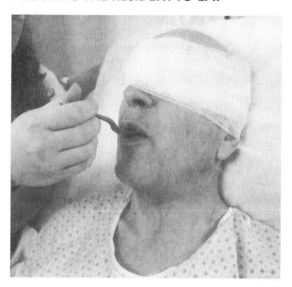

- Feed the resident slowly.
- Allow the resident to select the foods to be fed first.
- Cool the food by turning with the spoon.
- Season the food according to the resident's desire, following the appropriate diet.
- Tell the resident when you are offering hot liquids.
- Encourage independence during the meal.
- Fill the spoon half full using the spoon tip.

ASSISTING THE RESIDENT TO EAT

Use a straw to administer liquids if resident is able to tolerate a straw.

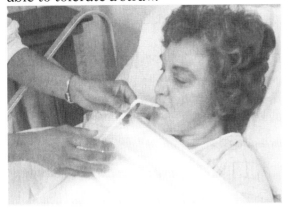

- Remove bedpans or urinals before meal is served.
- Always check the food tray for foods not allowed on the resident's diet.

1. Wash your hands before and after the procedure.
2. Greet the resident.
3. Check the armband.
4. Explain the procedure.
5. Wash his or her hands, and place the resident in a Fowler's position, if able.
6. Assemble the tray.
7. Recheck the armband with the tray card.
8. Provide privacy.
9. Explain to the resident which foods are on the tray.
10. Allow the resident to select the order of the food and to assist, if able.
11. Feed the resident slowly.
12. Tell the resident when offering hot liquids.
13. Allow the resident time to eat.
14. Calculate amount of food eaten.
15. Open the curtain.
16. Place the call signal within reach.
17. Assist the resident to a comfortable position.
18. Secure the resident.
19. Record and report the amount of food eaten and tolerance.

QUESTIONS

DIRECTIONS: Each question contains four suggested responses. Select the one best response to each question.

ANSWERS: See answers at the end of the questions.

1. All of the following nursing tasks are performed before serving the meal tray EXCEPT:
   a. Positioning the resident in a Fowler's position
   b. Washing the resident's hands
   c. Offering the bedpan or bathroom
   d. Placing the urinal on the bedside table

2. Select the first action of the nursing assistant before feeding the resident.
   a. Place the tray at the bedside.
   b. Wash your hands.
   c. Explain the procedure.
   d. Check the tray card.

3. All of the following nursing tasks are safety measures during the meal EXCEPT:
   a. Checking tray card with the armband.
   b. Elevating the head of the bed.
   c. Leaving a confused resident unattended.
   d. Checking the food tray.

4. Select the appropriate method to feed the helpless resident.
   a. Fill the spoon full with food.
   b. Place large amounts of food on the fork.
   c. Feed the resident using the side of the spoon.
   d. Fill the spoon half full and use the spoon tip.

5. Which one of the following actions by the nurse assistant would encourage independence while feeding the helpless resident?
   a. Hastily feed the resident.

b. Ask the resident how he or she would like to be fed.

c. Encourage a family member to feed the resident.

d. Tell the resident to feed him or herself.

6. All of the following tasks are performed by the nurse assistant during the feeding procedure EXCEPT:

a. Telling the resident the types of food on the tray

b. Feeding the resident slowly

c. Warning the resident if you are offering something hot.

d. Informing the resident that he or she must eat all of the food.

7. Which one of the following types of residents are at risk of choking during the meal.?

a. Totally dependent

b. Ambulatory

c. Self-care

d. Diabetic

8. Select the appropriate response of the nurse assistant if the resident refuses to eat.

a. Report to a family member.

b. Inform the charge nurse.

c. Encourage the resident to eat. If this is not effective, notify the charge nurse.

d. Verbally force the resident in a joking manner.

9. Pureed food is best described as:

a. Fried

b. Blended

c. Baked

d. Broiled

10. All of the following nursing tasks are performed after feeding the helpless resident EXCEPT:

a. Making the resident comfortable

b. Reporting and recording the amount of food consumed

c. Lowering the side rails

d. Placing the call signal within reach

Answers

1. d. The urinal should be rinsed and placed inside the bedside table. The resident's room should be free of unpleasant sights and odors.

2. b. Before beginning the feeding procedure, the nurse assistant should wash his or her hands.

3. c. Safety measures during the meal time are checking the tray card with the resident's armband, elevating the head of the bed if ordered, checking that the food tray agrees with diagnosis, and supervising the confused resident closely to prevent choking.

4. d. The appropriate method to feed the helpless resident is using a spoon and filling the spoon tip half full of food.

5. b. To encourage the resident's independence during the meal, ask the resident how he or she would like to be fed.

6. d. Informing the resident he or she must eat all of the food is not a part of the feeding procedure. Explaining the types of food, feeding the resident slowly and warning the resident if you offer something hot are the methods used.

7. a. Totally dependent residents are at a higher risk for choking. Many of these residents have difficulty chewing and swallowing.

8. c. If the resident refuses to eat, the nurse assistant should try to encourage the resident to eat. If this fails, report the problem to the charge nurse.

9. b. Pureed food is blended in the form of baby food. Residents with chewing and swallowing difficulties are likely to have a pureed diet ordered.

10. c. After completing the feeding procedure, the nurse assistant should make the resident comfortable, wash his or her face and hands, place the call signal within reach, raise the side rails, wash hands, and report and record observations.

22

Height and Weight Procedure

MEASURING THE HEIGHT AND WEIGHT

Using an Upright Scale

1. Wash your hands before and after the procedure.
2. Greet the resident.
3. Check the armband.
4. Explain the procedure.
5. Assist the resident to the scale.
6. Place a paper towel on the scale.
7. Assist the resident on the scale, facing away from the scale and lower the rod to the top of the head. Obtain the height.
8. Assist the resident to turn and face the scale.
9. Balance the scale and weigh the resident.
10. Assist the resident back to bed.
11. Secure the resident.
12. Place the call signal within reach.
13. Record and report observations to the charge nurse.

QUESTIONS

DIRECTIONS: Each question contains four suggested responses. Select the one best response to each question.

ANSWERS: See answers at the end of the chapter.

1. Select the *first* action of the nurse assistant before measuring the height and weight of the resident.
   a. Wash hands.
   b. Assemble your equipment.
   c. Explain the procedure.
   d. Provide privacy.

2. Which one of the following nursing tasks are performed after checking the resident's armband?
   a. Politely ask visitors to leave.
   b. Pull the curtain.
   c. Explain the procedure.
   d. Wash hands.

3. Select the most appropriate time at which the nurse assistant should measure the resident's height and weight.
   a. Admission
   b. Discharge
   c. Unit transfer
   d. Daily

4. All of the following tasks are performed before measuring the resident's weight and height EXCEPT:
   a. Balancing the scale to zero pounds
   b. Placing a paper towel on the scale
   c. Balancing the scale weights to 100 lbs
   d. Asking the resident to stand firmly on the scale

5. Select the appropriate method to determine an accurate weight using an upright scale.
   a. Balance the scale pointer toward the middle.
   b. Balance the scale pointer toward the top.
   c. Balance the scale pointer toward the bottom.

   d. Balance the bottom weights and estimate top weights.

6. Select the appropriate action of the nurse assistant after balancing the pointer on the upright scale.
   a. Add the number on the large balance only.
   b. Add the number on the small balance only.
   c. Estimate the resident's weight.
   d. Add the numbers on the larger and smaller balance.

7. In which direction should the nurse assistant position the resident to measure the height?
   a. Facing the scale
   b. Away from the scale
   c. Toward the right of the scale
   d. Toward the left of the scale

8. Select the correct position in which to place the measuring rod to measure the resident's height.
   a. Place gently on top of the resident's head.
   b. Place 1 inch above the head.
   c. Allow 1/2 inch for the resident's hair.
   d. Place two fingers between the resident's head and the rod.

9. All of the following actions ensure the resident's safety after completing the height and weight procedure EXCEPT:
   a. Allowing the resident to ambulate back to the room alone
   b. Assisting the resident back to the room
   c. Placing the call signal within reach
   d. Raising the side rails

10. Select the appropriate action by the nurse assistant after measuring the height and weight.
    a. Record the height and weight only.
    b. Notify the family.
    c. Notify the physician.
    d. Record and report the height and weight to the charge nurse.

MEASURING THE HEIGHT AND WEIGHT IN BED

Types of scales commonly used to weigh the resident on bed rest

- Bed scale
- Mechanical lift scale

Be sure to ask a coworker to assist, to ensure the safety of the resident.

1. Wash your hands before and after the procedure.
2. Greet the resident.
3. Check the armband.
4. Explain the procedure.
5. Assemble your equipment—tape measure, portable balance scale, bath blanket, note pad, and pen.
6. Provide privacy.

7. Cover the resident with a bath blanket.
8. Place the resident in a supine position.
9. Mark the sheet at the head and heel of the resident.
10. Reposition the resident to the side.
11. Measure the distance between the head and heels with the tape measure.
12. Record the height in inches, feet, or centimeters.
13. Place the bed scale on the bed, and balance the scale by standing the scale level with the bed.
14. Assist the resident to roll on the bed scale and adjust the scale to raise the resident slightly above the bed and obtain the weight.
15. Record the weight.
16. Remove the scale.
17. Assist the resident to a comfortable position.
18. Open the curtain.
19. Secure the resident.
20. Place the call signal within reach.
21. Wash your hands.
22. Record and report the observations to the charge nurse.

DIRECTIONS: Each question contains four suggested responses. Select the one best response to each question.

ANSWERS: See answers at the end of the chapter.

11. Select the **first** action of the nurse assistant before measuring the height of the resident in bed.
    a. Assemble your equipment.
    b. Explain the procedure.
    c. Provide privacy.
    d. Wash hands

12. In which one of the following positions should the nurse assistant place the resident to measure the height in bed?
    a. Fowler's
    b. Sims'
    c. Supine
    d. Prone

13. The supine position is best described as:
    a. Lying on the side
    b. Sitting upright in bed
    c. Lying face down
    d. Lying on the back

14. Select the action of the nurse assistant after placing the resident in the supine position.
    a. Place the tape measure on the forehead and measure downward.
    b. Mark the sheet at the ankles and neck area.
    c. Place the tape measure on the (L) great toe and measure upward.
    d. Mark the sheet at the head and heels of the resident

15. All of the following procedures are performed to measure a resident with a body contracture EXCEPT:
    a. Extending one arm at a right angle to the body
    b. Measuring from the center of the neck to the tip of the longest finger

    c. Multiplying the length result by 2 and subtracting 2 inches
    d. Estimating the height in feet and inches

16. All of the following are units of measure to document the resident's height EXCEPT:
    a. Fahrenheit degrees
    b. Feet
    c. Inches
    d. Centimeters

17. Select the appropriate method to balance the bed scale.
    a. Make sure the scale is standing level with the bed.
    b. Raise the bed higher than the scale.
    c. Lower the scale below the bed level.
    d. Elevate only the head of the bed only.

18. All of the following actions will ensure an accurate measurement of the resident's weight in bed EXCEPT:
    a. Asking a coworker to assist
    b. Placing the upper extremities toward the body
    c. Allowing a portion of the body to touch the mattress
    d. Raising all parts of the body off the mattress

19. An example of a safety measure to use while performing the height and weight procedure in bed is:
    a. Performing the procedure alone
    b. Asking a coworker to assist
    c. Keeping both side rails elevated
    d. Using your back muscles instead of thigh muscles for positioning

20. Which one of the following principles would include reporting the observations to the charge nurse?
    a. Independence
    b. Infections control
    c. Communications
    d. Dignity

Answers

1. a. The nurse assistant should perform hand-washing before measuring the weight and height of the resident.

2. c. The nurse assistant should explain the procedure to decrease the resident's apprehension.

3. a. The resident's height and weight are measured during the admission process. These measurements will be used for baseline measurements during the hospital stay and for future reference.

4. c. Balancing the scale weights to 100 lbs. is incorrect. The nurse assistant should balance the scale to zero, place a paper towel on the scale, and ask the resident to stand firmly on the scale.

5. a. To determine an accurate weight, the nurse assistant should balance the scale pointer toward the middle of the balance area on the upright scale.

6. d. After balancing the pointer on the upright scale, add the numbers on the large and small balances for a total weight.

7. b. The resident should be asked to position his or her body away from the height rod. The resident's heels should directly touch the measuring bar to obtain an accurate height.

8. a. The measuring rod should be placed gently on top of the resident's head.

9. a. Allowing the resident to ambulate back to the room alone is unsafe. The nurse assistant should ensure safety by assisting the resident back to the room, placing the call signal within reach and raising the side rails.

10. d. After measuring the height and weight, the nurse assistant should record and report the height and weight to the charge nurse.

11. d. Handwashing is the first action performed before measuring the resident's height in the bed.

12. c. The resident should be placed in a supine position.

13. d. A supine position is lying on the back.

14. d. Mark the sheet at the head and heels of the resident.

15. d. The nurse assistant should never estimate the height of the resident with contractures.

16. a. The Fahrenheit scale is used to measure the temperature. Correct units of measure to document the resident's height are inches, feet, and centimeters.

17. a. To balance the bed scale, the nurse assistant should position the bed scale level with the bed.

18. c. Allowing a portion of the resident's body to touch the bed will not ensure an accurate weight. Raising the entire body slightly above the mattress will ensure an accurate weight.

19. b. Asking a coworker to assist will ensure the safety of the resident. The coworker can support the resident during the procedure.

20. c. The principle of communications includes reporting the observations of the procedure to the charge nurse.

23

Range of Motion Procedure

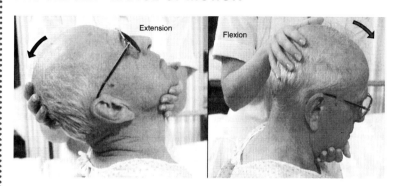

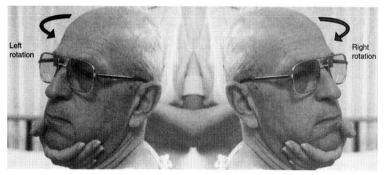

Head Exercises

- Do not give head excercises if the resident has a cervical injury

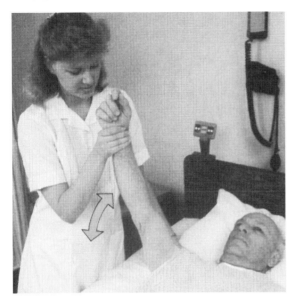

Flexion—raising the arm toward the resident's head.

Extension—lowering the arm toward the bed.

Internal and external rotation—moving the arm in a circular motion.

PROCEDURE: RANGE OF MOTION

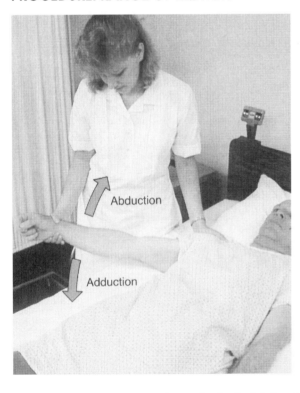

- Move the arm away from the body (abduction).
- Move the arm toward the body (adduction).

PROCEDURE: RANGE OF MOTION

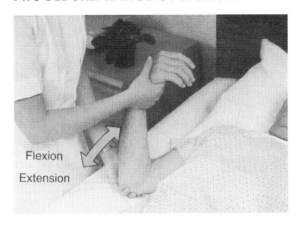

- Flexion is moving the elbow in an upward motion.
- Extension is moving the elbow in a downward motion.

PROCEDURE: RANGE OF MOTION

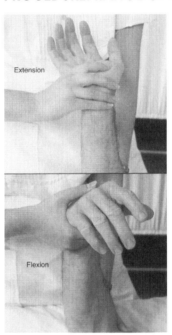

- Flexion is moving the wrist in a downward motion.

PROCEDURE: RANGE OF MOTION

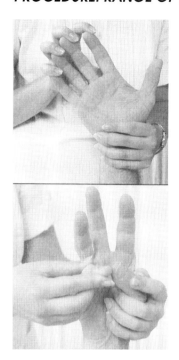

Exercise the fingers.

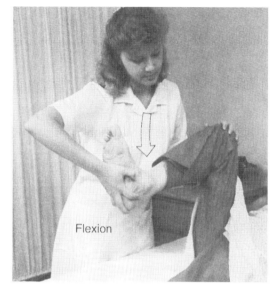

Flexion

- Knee joint flexion and extension

PROCEDURE: RANGE OF MOTION

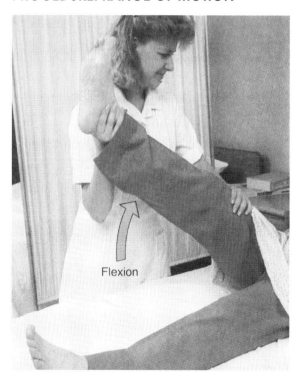

Flexion

- Exercise the leg

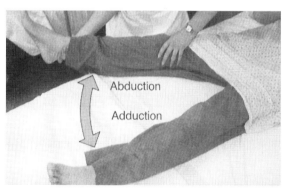

Abduction

Adduction

- Ankle joint Plantar flexion downward motion.

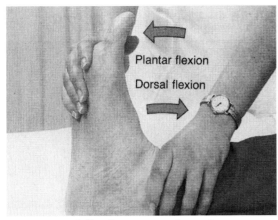

Plantar flexion

Dorsal flexion

- Dorsal flexion upward motion.
- Exercise each toe.

1. Wash your hands before and after the procedure.

2. Greet the resident.

3. Check the armband.

4. Explain the procedure.

5. Assemble your equipment—bath blanket.

6. Provide privacy.

7. Remove the covers and drape the resident with the bath blanket.

8. Exercise each joint three to five times. Remembering to use each exercise method. Begin with the head and move toward the toes. Validate pain level throughout the exercise, if extremely painful stop and report observations to the charge nurse.

9. Reposition the resident to a comfortable position.

10. Open the curtain.

11. Secure the resident.

12. Place the call signal within reach.

13. Record and report observations to the charge nurse.

QUESTIONS

DIRECTIONS: Each question contains four suggested responses. Select the one best response to each question.

ANSWERS: See answers at the end of the questions.

1. Range of motion is best described as:
   a. Movement of the resident's joints.
   b. Repositioning the resident's body.
   c. Transferring the resident to the chair.
   d. Assisting the resident to stand.

2. Select the first action of the nurse assistant before performing the range of motion procedure.
   a. Explain the procedure.
   b. Wash hands
   c. Pull the curtain.
   d. Lower the side rail.

3. When should the nurse assistant explain the range-of-motion procedure?
   a. During the procedure.
   b. After the procedure.
   c. Before the procedure.
   d. At no time.

4. Which one of the following exercise patterns are performed during the range-of-motion procedure?
   a. Move each joint at least three to five times.
   b. Move each joint one time.
   c. Move each joint two times.
   d. Move each joint seven to eight times.

5. Select the appropriate action of the nurse assistant to perform flexion.
   a. Move the elbow joint in an upward motion.
   b. Move the elbow joint in a downward motion.
   c. Rotate the elbow joint inward.
   d. Rotate the elbow joint outward.

6. Which one of the following movements should the nurse assistant understand regarding extension?
   a. Moving the elbow joint upward.
   b. Moving the elbow joint downward.
   c. Rotating the elbow joint inward.
   d. Rotating the elbow joint outward.

7. All of the following actions by the nurse assistant are appropriate during range-of-motion exercises EXCEPT:
   a. Allowing the resident to assist.
   b. Encouraging the resident to tolerate pain.
   c. Stopping the procedure if the exercise is too painful
   d. Exercising all the joints.

8. Select the appropriate action of the nurse assistant while exercising a right-hand contracture.
   a. Move the joint to the point of resistance.
   b. Severe contractures are exercised by the charge nurse.
   c. Stiff joints are not exercised.

   d. Move the joint past the point of resistance.

9. Select the appropriate information to report after the range of motion exercises are performed.
   a. Time and any complications.
   b. Tolerance and any contracture.
   c. Observations, tolerance, and time.
   d. Complaints of pain.

10. All of the following tasks are performed after the range of motion procedure EXCEPT:
    a. Handwashing
    b. Lowering the side rails
    c. Reporting and recording all observations
    d. Placing the call signal within reach

Answers

1. a. Range of motion is exercising the resident's joints. Range-of-motion procedures prevent contracture, strengthens muscles, and increase circulation.

2. b. The nurse assistant should perform handwashing prior to each procedure.

3. c. Explain the procedure before performing any procedure on the resident.

4. a. The joints are exercised at least three to five times each time range-of-motion exercises are performed.

5. a. Flexion is moving the elbow joint in an upward motion.

6. b. Extension is moving the elbow joint in a downward motion.

7. b. Encouraging a resident to tolerate pain during range-of-motion exercises is not appropriate.

8. a. The contracted joint is moved to the point of resistance. Never exercise the joint to the point of causing the resident pain.

9. c. Information the nurse assistant should report and record is the time of exercise, any observations during the exercise, and how the resident tolerated the range-of-motion exercise.

10. b. The nurse assistant should always elevate the side rail after each procedure, however, some residents may have a side rail release. Always review the resident's health record to verify all doctor's orders.

24

Diagrams of Commonly Used Positions

Supine position lying on the back.

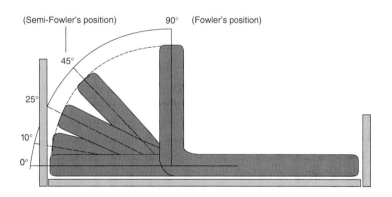

Low Fowler's, semi-Fowler's, and high Fowler's positions.

Prone position—lying on the abdomen

Left Sims'—lying on the left side; commonly used for the enema procedure.

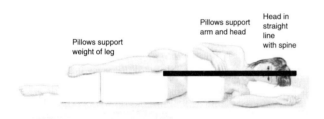

Left lateral—lying on the left side with the knee flexed.

Pillows support weight of leg

Pillows support arm and head

Head in straight line with spine

Place pillows in place for comfort.

Knee-chest position; commonly used for rectal examinations.

MOVING THE RESIDENT TO THE SIDE OF THE BED

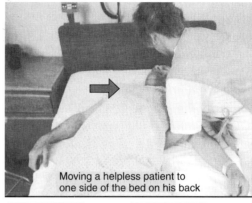

Moving a helpless patient to one side of the bed on his back

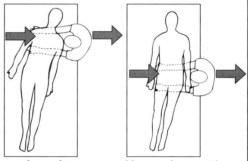

As a safety measure, this procedure must be done before turning a patient onto his side. It insures that the patient, when turned, is located in the center of the mattress.

Move the resident to the side of the bed in three sections: upper body, hips, and legs

MOVING THE RESIDENT UP IN THE BED USING A DRAW SHEET

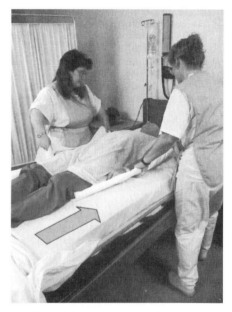

Each nurse assistant should stand on the opposite sides of the bed. Roll the draw sheet close to the resident's body; count 1, 2, and 3; move the resident on the count of 3.

1. Wash your hands before and after the procedure.

2. Greet the resident.

3. Check the armband.

4. Explain the procedure.

5. Assemble your equipment—bath blanket and pillows.

6. Provide privacy.

7. Follow the diagrams for desired positions and use pillows for comfort.

8. Assist the resident to a comfortable position.

9. Open the curtain.

10. Secure the resident.

11. Place the call signal within reach.

12. Record and report observations.

QUESTIONS

DIRECTIONS: Each question contains four suggested responses. Select the one best response to each question.

ANSWERS: See answers at the end of the questions.

1. Which one of the following positions best describe lying on the back with both legs together and extended?
   a. Fowler's
   b. Prone
   c. Knee-chest
   d. Supine

2. Which one of the following positions is likely to promote breathing?
   a. Prone
   b. Lateral
   c. Fowler's
   d. Sims'

3. Select the appropriate bed position in which the head of the bed is elevated to a 45° angle.
   a. Supine
   b. Semi-Fowler's
   c. High Fowler's
   d. Prone

4. The prone position is best described as:
   a. Lying on the abdomen
   b. Sitting upright in bed
   c. Lying on the back with the feet elevated
   d. Side lying

5. In which position should the nurse assistant place the resident to administer an enema?
   a. Sims'
   b. Fowler's
   c. Knee-chest
   d. Supine

6. The knee-chest position is best described as:
   a. Sitting upright with the knees flexed
   b. Lying face down with the knees flexed, and buttocks elevated
   c. Sitting on the side of the bed
   d. Lying face down with the legs extended

7. Which position is likely to cause pressure on the resident's hip area?
   a. Lateral
   b. Fowler's
   c. Supine
   d. Prone

8. Select the appropriate method to move the resident to the side of the bed.
   a. Assist the resident to a dangling position.
   b. Place one of the resident's legs across the other and turn.
   c. Move the resident in three sections.
   d. Apply the transfer belt and pull the resident.

9. Select the appropriate action of the nurse assistant to encourage the resident's cooperation during the positioning procedure.
   a. Explain the procedure before performing it.
   b. Encourage visitors to assist.
   c. Perform the procedure and explain it afterward.
   d. Verbally force the resident to cooperate.

10. Which one of the following methods should the nurse assistant perform to move the helpless resident up in bed with a coworkers assistance?

   a. Use a transfer belt.

   b. Lift the resident and move up in sections.

   c. Encourage the resident to pull up on the trapeze.

   d. Use the draw sheet.

Answers

1. d. The supine position is lying on the back with both legs together and extended.

2. c. To promote breathing, the resident is placed in a Fowler's position which is sitting upright in bed.

3. b. The semi-Fowler's position is elevating the head of the bed to a 45° angle.

4. a. The prone position is best described as lying on the abdomen with both legs extended.

5. a. The Sims' position is most commonly used to administer an enema.

6. b. The knee-chest position is lying face down with the buttocks elevated and the legs flexed.

7. a. The lateral position is lying on the side, causing the majority of the resident's weight to rest on the hip and shoulder areas. Problem areas should be monitored closely to prevent decubitus.

8. c. To move the resident to the side of the bed, the nurse assistant should move the resident in three sections. Move the upper body first and then the hips and legs.

9. a. An explanation of the positioning procedure will encourage the resident's cooperation.

10. d. The helpless resident is moved up in the bed, with the aid of two nurse assistants, by using the draw sheet.

25

Transferring the Resident Procedures

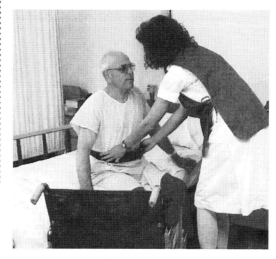

Transferring the resident from the bed to the wheelchair using a gait belt

Place the gait belt around the waist snug enough to allow two fingers between the gait belt and the resident's body

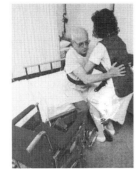
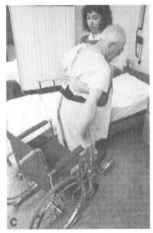
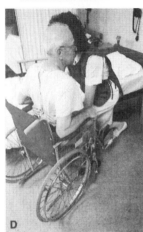

Transferring the resident from the bed to the wheelchair

- Place the chair on the unaffected side.
- Place the chair at a 45° angle.
- Lock the wheelchair for safety.
- Dangle the resident; check for dizziness.
- Assist the resident to stand holding the gait belt.
- Pivot the resident toward the chair.
- Gently lower the resident to the chair.
- Support the resident's weak side with pillows or an arm sling.

QUESTIONS

DIRECTIONS: Each question contains four suggested responses. Select the one best response to each question.

ANSWERS: See answers at the end of the chapter.

1. All of the following techniques are utilized to transfer the resident to the wheelchair EXCEPT:
   a. Body mechanics
   b. Draw sheet
   c. Pivot
   d. Transfer belt

2. Select the appropriate action of the nurse assistant to encourage the resident's cooperation during the transfer.
   a. Explain the procedure before the transfer.
   b. Discourage the resident's participation.
   c. Explain the procedure during the transfer.
   d. Allow a visitor to assist.

3. All of the following are appropriate actions of the nurse assistant if the resident refuses the transfer procedure EXCEPT:
   a. Encouraging the resident.
   b. Verbally threatening the resident.

c. Allowing the resident to refuse.
d. Reporting to the charge nurse.

4. At which one of the following angles should the nurse assistant position the wheelchair to transfer the resident?
   a. 20° angle.
   b. 35° angle.
   c. 45° angle.
   d. 60° angle.

5. Select the appropriate action of the nurse assistant after applying the gait belt.
   a. Immediately pull the resident to a standing position.
   b. Check the belt for a proper fit.
   c. Tell the resident to place his or her hands around your neck.
   d. Allow the transfer belt to hang loosely around the hips.

6. Which one of the following methods should the nurse assistant use to monitor the fit of the gait belt?
   a. Allow one finger space between the transfer belt and clothing.

b. Allow two finger spaces between the transfer belt and clothing.

c. Allow four finger spaces between the transfer belt and clothing.

d. Allow one fist space between the transfer belt and clothing.

7. Pivot is best described as:
   a. Assisting the resident to turn.
   b. Sitting on the side of the bed.
   c. Side lying.
   d. Sitting upright in the bed.

8. All of the following are performed after placing the resident in the wheelchair EXCEPT:
   a. Supporting the resident's weak side.
   b. Placing call signal within reach.
   c. Allowing the resident's weak side to hang freely.
   d. Removing the transfer belt.

9. How often should the nurse assistant perform handwashing during the transfer procedure?
   a. Before the procedure.
   b. After the procedure.
   c. Halfway through the procedure.
   d. Before and after the procedure.

10. Which one of the following observations should be reported immediately after placing the resident in the wheelchair?
    a. Coughing.
    b. Shortness of breath.
    c. Sneezing.
    d. Warm skin.

TRANSFERRING THE RESIDENT FROM THE BED TO THE STRETCHER

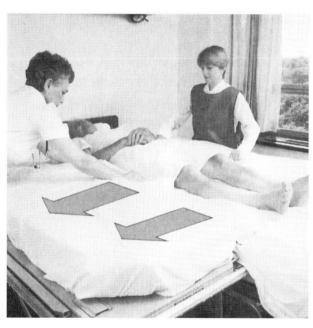

- Raise the bed to the level of the stretcher.

- Lock the wheels on the stretcher and the bed.

- Position your body against the stretcher; ask a coworker to stand on the opposite side of the bed to support the resident.

- Roll the draw sheet close to the resident's body.

- Count one, two, three; on three, pull the resident onto the stretcher.

- Secure the straps on the stretcher and raise the side rails for safety.

- Cover the resident.

QUESTIONS

DIRECTIONS: Each question contains four suggested responses. Select the one best response to each question.

ANSWERS: See answers at the end of the chapter.

11. All of the following are actions of the nurse assistant during the transfer from the bed to the stretcher procedure EXCEPT:
   a. Assembling the equipment.
   b. Handwashing.
   c. Checking the armband.
   d. Transferring the resident alone.

12. Which one of the following methods would promote the resident's cooperation during the transfer procedure?
   a. Allow a visitor to assist.
   b. Explain the procedure.
   c. Tell the resident not to worry.
   d. Use a transfer belt.

13. Select the appropriate position to transfer a helpless resident from the bed to the stretcher.
   a. Fowler's.
   b. Prone.
   c. Supine.
   d. Lateral.

14. Select the appropriate bed height to perform the transfer from the bed to stretcher procedure.
   a. Higher than the stretcher.
   b. Height of the bed doesn't matter.
   c. Lower than the stretcher.
   d. Level with the stretcher.

15. All of the following safety measures are performed during the bed to stretcher transfer procedure EXCEPT:
   a. Elevating the side rail on one side of the bed.
   b. Locking the wheels on the bed.
   c. Using your body to hold the bed in place.
   d. Locking the wheels on the stretcher.

16. Select the appropriate safety aid to transfer the resident from the bed to the stretcher.
   a. Transfer belt
   b. Draw sheet
   c. Egg crate mattress
   d. Trapeze bar

17. All of the following are methods to transfer the resident using a draw sheet EXCEPT:
   a. Standing with the feet 12 inches apart
   b. Rolling the draw sheet close to the resident's body
   c. Moving the resident in three sections
   d. Counting "one, two, three" and lifting

18. All of the following nursing measures are performed after transferring the resident to the stretcher EXCEPT:
   a. Supporting the head and feet, if allowed
   b. Covering the resident with a sheet or blanket
   c. Fastening the stretcher straps
   d. Raising one side rail on the stretcher

19. How often should the nurse assistant perform handwashing during the bed to stretcher transfer procedure?
   a. Not at all
   b. Once
   c. Twice
   d. Three times

20. Select the appropriate action of the nurse assistant after the completion of the bed to stretcher transfer procedure.
   a. Report the completion of the procedure to the charge nurse.
   b. Record the procedure at the end of the shift.
   c. Ask another nurse assistant to record the procedure.
   d. Take a break and report the procedure later.

ASSISTING THE RESIDENT WITH AMBULATION, WITH OR WITHOUT THE WALKER, USING A GAIT OR TRANSFER BELT

Assisting the Resident with Ambulation

Hold the gait belt from the back for balance

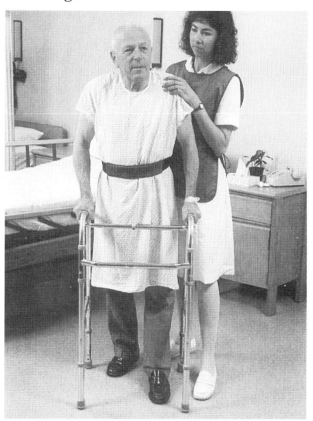

Encourage the resident to use a walker for support

1. Wash your hands before and after the procedure.
2. Greet the resident.
3. Check the armband.
4. Explain the procedure.
5. Assemble your equipment—transfer belt and walker.
6. Pull the curtain.
7. Lock the wheels on the bed.
8. Lower the height of the bed.
9. Dress the resident appropriately, including nonskid shoes.
10. Assist the resident to a dangling position.
11. Apply the transfer belt for support and safety.
12. Stand in front of the resident.
13. Using good body mechanics, assist the resident to stand, ask the resident if he or she is okay.
14. Hold the transfer belt from the back, and allow the resident to use the walker, if ordered.
15. Ambulate the resident while supporting the shoulder and ambulating to the side of the resident.
16. Be sure to ask the resident if dizziness or severe weakness is present. If the resident complains of dizziness or severe weakness, return the resident to bed.
17. Make the resident comfortable.
18. Raise the side rails for safety.
19. Open the curtain.
20. Place the call signal within reach.
21. Return your equipment to the proper place.
22. Wash your hands.
23. Record and report observations to the charge nurse.

QUESTIONS

DIRECTIONS: Each question contains four suggested responses. Select the one best response to each question.

ANSWERS: See answers at the end of the chapter.

21. Select the *first* action of the nurse assistant before assisting the resident to ambulate.
    a. Explain the procedure.
    b. Perform the handwashing procedure.
    c. Check the identification bracelet.
    d. Assemble the equipment.

22. All of the following are performed before the ambulation procedure EXCEPT:
    a. Handwashing.
    b. Checking the identification bracelet.
    c. Asking any visitors to assist.
    d. Explain the procedure.

23. Select the appropriate method to prevent a violation of the resident's dignity while assisting the resident to ambulate.
    a. Refer to the resident as "honey."
    b. Address the resident by his or her name.
    c. Refer to the resident as "gramps."
    d. Refer to the resident as "sweetheart."

24. All of the following are safety methods performed before assisting the resident to ambulate EXCEPT:
    a. Allowing the resident to stand alone.
    b. Lowering the height of the bed.
    c. Applying a transfer belt.
    d. Locking the wheels on the bed.

25. Dangle is best described as:
    a. Sitting upright in bed.
    b. Sitting on the side of the bed.
    c. Lying in bed with the head elevated 45°.
    d. Standing at the side of the bed.

26. Select the appropriate method to apply the transfer belt.
    a. Apply loosely around the hips.
    b. Apply tightly around the waist.
    c. Allow two finger spaces under the transfer belt.
    d. Allow four finger spaces under the transfer belt.

27. Which one of the following actions of the nurse assistant is performed while assisting the resident to ambulate?
    a. Hold the transfer belt from the back.
    b. Hold the transfer belt at the side.
    c. Hold the resident's hand.
    d. Hold the resident around the shoulder.

28. Select the appropriate response if the resident complains of dizziness while ambulating with assistance.
    a. Tell the resident not to think about dizziness.
    b. Offer the resident a glass of water.
    c. Ask the resident to try to complete the exercise.
    d. Return the resident to bed immediately.

29. All of the following are appropriate actions of the nurse assistant regarding a resident's refusal of the ambulation procedure EXCEPT:
    a. Allowing the resident the right of refusal.
    b. Informing the resident that he or she must participate.
    c. Reporting the incident to the charge nurse.
    d. Encouraging the resident's participation.

30. Select the appropriate information to report and record after assisting the resident to ambulate.
    a. Tolerance and time.
    b. Unusual observations only.
    c. Distance, tolerance, time, and observations.
    d. Time and distance.

Answers

1. b. Body mechanics, pivot foot motion, and a gait belt are utilized to transfer a resident safely. The draw sheet is used while the resident is being repositioned in the bed.

2. a. An explanation of the procedure will inform the resident and encourage the resident's cooperation.

3. b. The nurse assistant should allow the resident to refuse, and should politely encourage the resident to participate. If the resident refuses after encouragement, report the refusal to the charge nurse. Never verbally threaten the resident to receive any procedure. The resident has the right to refuse.

4. c. The wheelchair is placed at a 45° angle to allow a smooth transfer.

5. b. The nurse assistant should check the gait belt for a proper fit directly after application.

6. b. To monitor the fit of the transfer belt the nurse assistant should allow two finger spaces between the transfer belt and the resident's clothing.

7. a. Pivot is best described as assisting the resident to slowly turn by guiding the resident's feet and body.

8. c. The resident's weak side should be supported on pillows or placed in a sling. Never allow the weak side to hang freely.

9. d. The nurse assistant should perform handwashing before and after each procedure.

10. b. The inability to breathe is a life-threatening situation and should be reported immediately to the charge nurse.

11. d. The nurse assistant should assemble the equipment, wash hands, check the resident's identification armband and ask a coworker to assist with the bed to stretcher transfer.

12. b. An explanation of the transfer procedure will promote the resident's cooperation.

13. c. The supine position is the appropriate position to transfer the helpless resident from the bed to the stretcher.

14. d. The bed is elevated to the level of the stretcher to perform the bed to stretcher transfer procedure.

15. a. Both of the side rails are lowered to perform the bed to stretcher transfer procedure.

16. b. A draw sheet is utilized to transfer the resident from the bed to the stretcher.

17. c. The nurse assistant should stand with feet 12 inches apart, roll the draw sheet close to the resident's body, count "one, two, three," and lift and move the resident's body together with a coworker.

18. d. Both side rails on the stretcher should be elevated. Raising both of the side rails will prevent the resident from falling.

19. c. Handwashing is performed before and after the transfer procedure.

20. a. After completing the bed to stretcher transfer procedure, the nurse assistant should report all observations to the charge nurse.

21. b. Perform the handwashing procedure before assisting the resident to ambulate.

22. c. Don't ask any visitors to assist with the ambulation procedure. Politely ask the visitors to step out of the room.

23. b. Always address or call the resident by his or her name. Never address the resident as "Sweetie," "Honey," "Gramps," or "Grandma." This is disrespectful.

24. a. Don't allow the resident to stand alone. You must support the resident to ensure safety.

25. b. Dangle is best described as sitting the resident on the side of the bed.

26. c. Apply the transfer belt allowing two finger spaces between the transfer belt and the clothing.

27. a. The transfer belt should be held from the back to allow for more support.

28. d. If the resident complains of dizziness during the ambulation procedure, return the resident to bed immediately. Monitor the vital signs and report observations to the charge nurse.

29. b. The resident has the right of refusal. Never inform a resident that he or she must participate. Encourage the resident, to participate; if this is ineffective, report the incident to the charge nurse.

30. c. The nurse assistant should report and record the resident's tolerance, distance, time, and unusual observations.

26

Applying the Elastic Bandage and Anti-Embolism Elastic Stocking Procedure

APPLICATION OF ELASTIC BANDAGES

- Use two circular turns to secure the bandage.
- Keep the bandage smooth.
- Overlap the bandage edges to cover the area and to prevent the bandage from sliding.
- Expose the fingers or toes to monitor circulation.
- Secure the elastic bandage with clips or velcro.

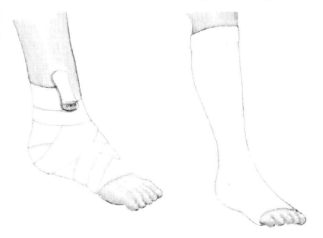

Apply the elastic bandage upward, in the direction of the blood flow.

APPLICATION OF ANTIEMBOLISM STOCKINGS

- Correct fit.
- Apply while the resident is lying down.
- Remove every 8 hours and reapply per physician's order.
- Remove all wrinkles.

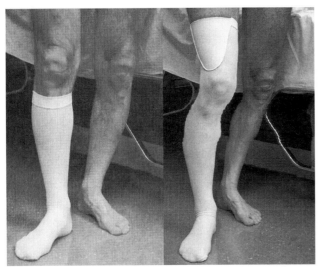

Two types of antiembolism stocking; knee length and full length

1. Wash your hands before and after the procedure.

2. Greet the resident.

3. Check the armband.

4. Explain the procedure.

5. Assemble your equipment—elastic bandage or anti-embolism stocking.

6. Provide privacy.

7. Application of the elastic bandage should begin with a double circular wrap to secure the bandage. Apply the bandage in the direction of the blood flow toward the heart. Overlap the bandage to prevent sliding and to cover the area. Allow the fingers or toes to be exposed to monitor circulation. Secure the bandage with a clip or velcro.

8. Anti-embolism stocking application should be with the resident lying in bed. Apply the stocking without leaving any wrinkles. Roll the stocking upward, making sure the stocking fits the leg to ensure the proper compression action.

9. Assist the resident to a comfortable position.

10. Open the curtain.

11. Secure the resident.

12 Place the call signal within reach.

13. Record and report observations to the charge nurse.

QUESTIONS

DIRECTIONS: Each question contains four suggested responses. Select the one best response to each question.

ANSWERS: See answers at the end of the questions.

1. Select the first action of the nurse assistant before applying the elastic bandage.
   a. Wash hands.
   b. Explain the procedure.
   c. Assemble your equipment.
   d. Check the armband.

2. All of the following are nursing tasks performed before the application of the elastic bandage EXCEPT:
   a. Identification of the resident.
   b. Handwashing.
   c. Explanation of procedure.
   d. Recording the procedure.

3. Select the appropriate response of the nurse assistant if the resident refuses the prescribed procedure.
   a. Verbally force the resident to be cooperative.
   b. Encourage the resident to cooperate. If this is ineffective, report the incident.
   c. Allow the resident to refuse without discussion.
   d. Refuse to perform any further care.

4. Select the appropriate method to apply the elastic bandage.
   a. Apply the bandage in the direction toward the heart.
   b. Apply the bandage in an upward and downward direction.

c. Apply the bandage in the direction away from the heart.

d. Apply the bandage loosely with a portion of skin exposed.

5. Which one of the following methods should the nurse assistant understand regarding observations after the application of an elastic bandage.

a. Wrap the bandage loosely allowing skin exposure.

b. Allow exposure of the toes to monitor skin changes.

c. Feel the bandage to monitor skin changes.

d. Remove elastic bandages every 2 hours to check circulation.

6. Select the appropriate position of the resident for applying the elastic stocking (anti-embolism).

a. Lying in bed.

b. Dangling.

c. Sitting in the chair.

d. Standing.

7. How often should the nurse assistant remove and reapply the elastic stocking?

a. Every 2 hours.

b. Every 4 hours.

c. Every 6 hours.

d. Every 8 hours.

8. To which one of the following types of residents would the nurse assistant likely apply elastic stockings?

a. Psychiatric.

b. Obstetric.

c. Surgical.

d. Pediatric.

9. All of the following nursing tasks are performed after the completion of the application of elastic bandages EXCEPT:

a. Placing the call signal within reach.

b. Handwashing.

c. Opening the curtain.

d. Lowering the side rails.

10. Select the last action of the nurse assistant after completing the application of the elastic bandage procedure.

a. Wash hands.

b. Report and record observations.

c. Place the call signal within reach.

d. Record abnormal observations.

Answers

1. a. The first action of the nurse assistant before applying the elastic bandage is to perform handwashing.

2. d. Recording the procedure is performed after completing the elastic bandage procedure.

3. b. The nurse assistant should encourage the resident in a polite manner, if this is ineffective, report the incident to your charge nurse.

4. a. The elastic bandage is applied in the direction toward the heart.

5. b. Allow exposure of the toes to monitor skin changes.

6. a. The resident should be lying in bed before applying the elastic stockings.

7. d. The anti-embolism elastic stocking should be removed and reapplied every 8 hours.

8. c. The nurse assistant would likely apply the elastic stocking to the postoperative or surgical resident. Anti-embolism elastic stockings are also applied to residents with thrombophlebitis or phlebitis.

9. d. The nurse assistant should always elevate the resident's side rails for safety.

10. b. The last action of the nurse assistant is to report and record all observations during the application of the elastic bandage procedure.

27

Restraints

- Physician's order must be obtained before application.

- Allow two finger spaces between the vest and the clothing to ensure proper fit.

- Check every 30 minutes for normal skin tone.

- Remove the vest restraint every 2 hours for 10 minutes to allow movement.

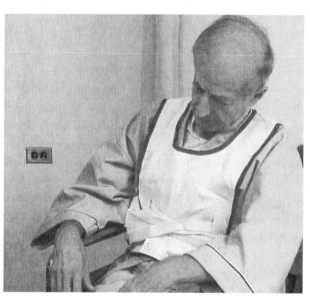

Make sure the vest is not stopping the circulation.

1. Wash your hands before and after the procedure.

2. Greet the resident.

3. Explain the procedure.

4. Assemble your equipment—vest restraint.

5. Provide privacy.

6. Place the vest opening toward the back. Be sure to crisscross the vest straps and secure with an easy to

release tie under the bed or wheelchair frame.

7. Place two fingers between the vest and clothing to ensure proper fit. Check the resident every 30 minutes for normal skin tones. Remove the restraint every 2 hours for 10 minutes to allow movement.

8. Open the curtain.

9. Place the call signal within reach.

10. Record and report observations to the charge nurse.

QUESTIONS

DIRECTIONS: Each question contains four suggested responses. Select the one best response to each question.

ANSWERS: See answers at the end of the questions.

1. Which one of the following team members can authorize the application of a vest restraint?
   a. Nurse assistant.
   b. Physical therapist.
   c. Charge nurse.
   d. Occupational therapist

2. Select the appropriate action of the nurse assistant before placing a vest restraint on a resident.
   a. Explain the procedure.
   b. Assemble your equipment.
   c. Lower the side rail.
   d. Place the call signal in reach.

3. How often should the nurse assistant perform handwashing during the application of a vest restraint procedure?
   a. Before the procedure only
   b. After the curtain is closed
   c. Before the equipment is assembled
   d. Before and after the procedure

4. Select the appropriate nursing principle to encourage the resident's cooperation before applying the vest restraint.
   a. Independence
   b. Safety
   c. Communications
   d. Privacy

5. All of the following are methods to apply the vest restraint EXCEPT:
   a. Applying the vest restraint beneath the clothing.
   b. Placing the solid area of the vest restraint toward the front.
   c. Crisscrossing the straps in the back.
   d. Bringing the loose ends of the straps through the holes toward the front.

6. Which method should the nurse assistant perform to check for fit and comfort of the vest restraint?
   a. Allow one finger space between the vest restraint and the resident's body.
   b. Allow two finger spaces between the vest restraint and the resident's body.
   c. Allow four finger spaces between the vest restraint and the resident's body.
   d. Allow one fist space between the vest restraint and the resident's body.

7. Select the appropriate area on the bed to secure the vest restraint straps.
   a. Head of the bed
   b. Side rail bar
   c. Mattress
   d. Bed frame

8. Select the appropriate area on the wheelchair to secure the vest restraint straps.
   a. Back frame
   b. Brake bar
   c. Arm rest
   d. Wheel rim

9. All of the following are monitoring methods for the resident wearing the vest restraint EXCEPT:
   a. Rechecking the resident every 30 minutes.
   b. Observing the skin for color and temperature.

c. Removing the restraint every 2 hours and exercising the resident.

d. Releasing the restraint straps every 4 hours.

10. Select the last action of the nurse assistant after applying the vest restraint.
    a. Wash hands.
    b. Place the call signal within reach.
    c. Report and record observations.
    d. Raise the side rail.

Answers

1. c. The application of a vest restraint can be authorized by your immediate supervisor or charge nurse. A written order from the physician should be in the resident's health record.

2. b. Assemble your equipment before applying the vest restraint.

3. d. Handwashing is performed before and after the procedure.

4. c. The principle of communications will encourage cooperation. Explaining the procedure to the resident will allow the resident to feel less apprehensive and be more cooperative.

5. a. The vest restraint is placed over the resident's clothing. Placing the vest restraint over the clothing will prevent friction and direct pressure on the skin surface.

6. b. Allow two finger spaces between the vest restraint and the resident's body.

7. d. The vest restraint straps are secured to the bed frame. Never secure the restraint straps to the side rails on the bed.

8. a. The vest restraint straps are secured to the wheelchair back frame beneath the seat.

9. d. Releasing the vest restraint straps every 4 hours is not a monitoring method. The nurse assistant should recheck the resident every 30 minutes, observe the skin for color and temperature, remove the restraint every 2 hours, offer bed pan or urinal, offer fluids, give skin care, and exercise the resident.

10. c. The last nursing task performed after application of the vest restraint is reporting and recording observations.